Bluebirds
—— and ——
Their Survival

Bluebirds
—— and ——
Their Survival

Wayne H. Davis
Philippe Roca

THE UNIVERSITY PRESS OF KENTUCKY

Editorial and Sales Offices: Lexington, Kentucky 40508-4008

Library of Congress Cataloging-in-Publication Data

Davis, Wayne Harry, 1930–
   Bluebirds and their survival / Wayne H. Davis and Philippe Roca.
      p.   cm.
   Includes bibliographical references (p.   ) and index
   ISBN 0-8131-0846-2 (acid-free paper)
   1. Bluebirds. 2. Bird attracting. 3. Bluebirds—Housing.
4. Birds, Protection of.   I. Roca, Philippe, 1956–   . II. Title.
QL696.P288D38   1995
639.9'78842—dc20   94-45681

7/95 Ingram 14.36

Contents

Figures

Preface

BLUEBIRDS ARE ONE of the most beloved birds among people who are familiar with them. Unfortunately, most Americans have never seen one. Bluebirds are almost entirely dependent upon people and thus are usually seen only in places where people have erected nest boxes for them. Fortunately, they are one of the easiest birds to attract, and many people get pleasure from providing nest sites and monitoring the progress of their birds.

Several books on bluebirds are in print, and each provides valuable information. They all encourage people to build boxes, to establish trails, and to become more familiar with these delightful birds while helping to increase their population. Various authors provide a wealth of information on the problems one might encounter and on solutions to these problems.

Building and maintaining a bluebird trail should be easy and fun. We believe that many books on the topic make things more complicated than necessary. Some books recommend nest boxes that, data show, bluebirds do not like. The design most favored by bluebirds, the Peterson box, is needlessly complicated to build, and it is also a haven for house sparrows. The box requires an excessive amount of lumber, and starlings may also be attracted to it.

Other writers place undue stress on the predator problem and advocate too much effort to eliminate it. Some writers and some bluebird societies insist that no box should be put up unless it is equipped with a predator guard. Evidence suggests, however, that the various guards attached to boxes are more effective at deterring bluebirds than predators. To make a site permanently predator-proof requires extra effort, which in some cases is worthwhile; however, our philosophy is that one should not be too concerned about native predators. The operator of a bluebird trail will have an opportunity to become acquainted with a variety of wildlife and to develop an appreciation for our native natural world. In spite of some predation, a trail of boxes will produce many new bluebirds.

We've tried to weed through the rumors and anecdotes and offer advice that has been tested and has achieved positive results. We can't guarantee that with this book you'll have success attracting and raising bluebirds. It will, however, most certainly help you tip the odds in your favor.

Except for chapter 12, Photographing Birds, which was written by Philippe Roca, the text in this book has been written by Wayne H. Davis. All photographs are the work of Philippe Roca.

Acknowledgments

We thank Beverly Lovaas for help with some of the drawings and the North American Bluebird Society for funding some of our bluebird research at the University of Kentucky. Philippe Roca extends special thanks to Janine and George in Saint-Aigulin and Bert and Millie in Maceo.

Introduction

WHEN I WAS A BOY in Morgantown, West Virginia, in the 1930s, a pair of eastern bluebirds *(Sialia sialis)* nested beside my elementary school. The nest site was a cavity in a small dead branch that had been excavated by a downy woodpecker in the backyard of a home. The foraging territory for the bluebirds was the school playground, a small area suitable only for a single pair. They nested there for two seasons and were never seen again. They may have been the last pair to nest at the site. Bluebirds have abandoned the cities and suburbs, leaving these areas to the introduced house sparrows *(Passer domesticus)* and European starlings *(Sturnus vulgaris)*, which compete with them for nest sites. Bluebirds are easily driven from a nest site by these aggressive foreign intruders.

Bluebird populations are growing.

In my childhood days, I built wren houses and put them up on our property, locating them carefully around the edges to see how many different territories I could establish on our several city lots. I got the pattern from an old bird book that suggested dimensions and entrance sizes for various species that would nest in cavities. I was intrigued by the design for a bluebird house and asked my father to get us an inch-and-a-half auger bit so I could build one.

To my great disappointment, my father said that it was no use to build a bluebird house because it would only be taken over by house sparrows, and we did not want to provide nest sites for those pests. He told me that when he was a boy, he and his neighbors had bluebird houses right in the front yard. Bluebirds would even nest on the porch if a suitable cavity were available. As house sparrows became more abundant, however, the bluebirds left, and people sadly came to realize that the days of the bluebirds on the front lawn apparently were gone. Although starlings, which are bigger than bluebirds, can be excluded from a nest box, any cavity accessible to bluebirds can also be used by the smaller house sparrow.

Growing up in the city with an intense interest in birds and their nesting habits, I became thoroughly familiar with the varied nest site selections of house sparrows. I soon found that their favored sites were crevices in buildings or spaces behind signs that were high enough to be beyond my reach. If no crevice were available, they would sometimes build bulky nests in an evergreen or dense thorn tree, but always well beyond my reach. The few times I did get access to a nest site, I found that the sparrows would, whenever possible, go deep into a crevice where the eggs and young were still beyond my reach.

I also noticed that out in the country in pasture lands, bluebirds were still rather common. They nested in cavities in fence posts, and I was fortunate enough to find several of these sites. I observed a nest where the birds entered a knothole in a post so badly weathered that a split on the opposite side was large enough that I could easily look in and see the young. Another site was a hollowed center on the top of the fence post. Not only were the young quite visible, but they were completely exposed to the rain. Still another nest site was a place where a person had put an old 1940s-style coffee can on top of a fence post. This broad shallow can was inverted on the post but did not come down on it very far. A flaw at one place on the post provided just enough room for a bluebird to enter. The nest was under the can on top of the post. Even as a young boy I was aware that none of these sites would be of interest to house sparrows. The coffee can was near a house and barn where sparrows were abundant, yet the bluebirds were unmolested.

As the years went by the old wooden fence posts were gradually replaced across the nation with steel posts or wooden posts pressure-treated with creosote, and the nest sites for bluebirds gradually but steadily decreased. Bluebirds became scarce and became almost entirely dependent upon people who built houses for them in hopes that a brood or two could be raised before the sparrows took over.

For several decades I spent the bulk of my professional career as a student of bats and other small mammals. In the 1960s and 1970s, as an avocation, I began playing with the problem of bluebirds and house sparrows during summer vacations in Minnesota, basing my efforts on my childhood knowledge of the subtle differences in the nest site requirements of the two species.

In the 1980s I began a serious effort to solve the house sparrow problem. In a series of experiments at the University of Kentucky, with the financial aid of the North American Bluebird Society, I have been trying to develop a nest box and site choices favorable to bluebirds but of no interest to house sparrows. I've made considerable progress. On the University livestock farms, where house sparrows are abundant—far more common than bluebirds—we have placed boxes that are much more likely to attract bluebirds than sparrows. We have bluebirds raising families near farm buildings and livestock feeding areas unmolested by the numerous house sparrows.

Cast of Characters

Bluebirds are in the thrush family, a group that includes our robin, several magnificent North American songsters, and the European nightingale. The bluebird subfamily is restricted to North America. It consists of three species: the eastern bluebird *(Sialia sialis)*, the west-

Eastern bluebird

ern bluebird *(Sialia mexicana)*, and the mountain bluebird *(Sialia currucoides)*. Except for parts of Alaska, bluebirds breed in all parts of all the continental United States, wherever suitable habitat and nest sites occur. Although the three species are usually separated geographically there is some overlap of range, and in western Montana all are found. All three species have similar requirements, and all will nest in boxes provided for them.

The eastern bluebird ranges throughout the eastern states, westward across the Great Plains to the foot of the Rockies and across southern Canada from Nova Scotia to Alberta. The adult male is a beautiful iridescent blue with an orange breast and white belly. The female appears gray, but closer observation shows blue in the tail and wing feathers and a pale orange breast. The young are a rather plain gray with a speckled breast and some blue in the wing and tail feathers.

The western bluebird ranges in the pinon-juniper and ponderosa pines at elevations of five to six thousand feet in the Rocky Mountains. Westward to the Pacific coast and into southern British Columbia they occur at lower elevations. The adult male differs in appearance from the eastern bluebird by his blue throat and a russet patch across the back. The female and young have gray throats and are more brownish than eastern bluebirds.

The mountain bluebird ranges from central Alaska southward in the mountains to New Mexico, Arizona, and California. In the southern part of its range it usually occurs at elevations above five thousand feet, ranging to thirteen thousand feet. It ranges eastward in Canada across the prairie provinces and has recently extended its range into northwestern Minnesota. The extensive nest box trail across Canada has likely been responsible for this change.

The adult male mountain bluebird is solid blue. Neither sex has any russet; the female has a gray breast. This species is slightly larger than the other two. People who have experience with mountain bluebirds recommend a circular entrance to the box of 1⁹/₁₆ inches in diameter instead of the usual 1½ inches for other bluebirds (Hagerman 1988). A slot entrance should be 30 mm high. Mountain bluebirds average larger broods than eastern bluebirds and perhaps should have a more roomy box (Rounds and Monroe 1983).

The eastern and western bluebirds are closely related species that apparently developed from a single species when the Ice Age pushed them into separate refugia of what is now Florida and Mexico. In this they follow tanagers, grosbeaks, buntings, and others in which there are closely related species east and west. The evolutionary derivation of the mountain bluebird remains a mystery.

1

Bluebird Habitat

BLUEBIRDS FEED on the ground and must have access to insects that they can see from a perch or by hovering. They must have open land; they will not nest in the forest or in dense brushy areas.

A parklike stand of trees is satisfactory if the ground is covered with grass that is mowed or grazed. Most pastureland makes excellent habitat. Golf courses, lawns, and orchards are suitable. The right-of-ways along interstate highways, freeways, and toll roads provide

Bluebird habitat

Bluebird habitat

excellent habitat; boxes mounted on right-of-way fence posts attract bluebirds.

Land surface-mined for coal or other minerals provides some of the best habitat we have found; our experimental boxes on such lands in Kentucky sometimes get 100 percent occupancy by bluebirds. Boxes placed on bare, newly mined ground are used, as are those on lands reclaimed to herbaceous vegetation that is neither mowed nor grazed. Parking lots and campgrounds at state parks and other such recreation areas provide good bluebird habitat.

Some croplands provide suitable habitat if not sprayed and devoid of insects. Land with dense crops, such as corn, wheat and soybeans, is not suitable for bluebirds. Weed fields are satisfactory if plants are not so dense as to exclude access to the ground.

Bluebirds like to have a perch from which they can view the ground looking for insects. Utility lines overhead definitely increase the quality of a site; a fence or tree is satisfactory. A perch site is not essential, however; we have had bluebirds nest on the mines, where

Bluebird habitat

the only perch within half a mile was the box and the steel post on which it was mounted.

In winter the habitat shifts somewhat. Although still to be found foraging in open land, bluebirds will retreat to the cover of woods and brushy areas, where they would not be seen in summer. The trees that make up the forest edge are a favored place in winter.

2

Boxes and Other Nest Structures

IN RECENT YEARS, bluebirds have become ever more dependent upon people to provide nest sites; today probably the majority are raised in boxes built and erected for them by interested people. Zeleny's (1976) book on the plight of the bluebird and the establishment of the North American Bluebird Society in 1979 led to widespread interest in providing satisfactory homes for the bluebirds and thus a resurgence of the much diminished population.

Bluebirds, like purple martins, are nearly domestic. Several times I have had a pair watch me erect a nest box and come down to inspect it as I was walking away. They seem to expect people to provide nest sites, and they do not object to one's checking on their nesting progress. Bluebirds will often sit peacefully on a wire and watch a person open a box to inspect their nest. Sometimes an incubating female will sit tight while the box is opened and closed. Most bird species will abandon eggs if disturbed, but I have never had bluebirds abandon a box at any stage because of human disturbance. It seems as if the bluebirds are aware that a person is checking on their welfare.

Bluebirds will nest in a wide variety of containers of various dimensions. They apparently prefer wooden boxes over other material (Davis 1989a). A standard box is one with an entrance 1½ inches (38 mm) in diameter, about seven inches (175 mm) above the floor, with floor dimensions of 4 x 4 inches (10 cm). Such a box is readily used by bluebirds. Houses of this design, however, are strongly favored by house sparrows, which are quite likely to take them over. We do not recommend placing them anywhere this pest is found unless you plan to control house sparrows by trapping them.

A simple nest box can be made from a half-gallon milk carton or a plastic gallon jug of the type used for vinegar, bleach, windshield washer, and antifreeze. We provide directions for this type of box in chapter 11. Although house wrens (*Troglodytes acedon*), Carolina chickadees (*Parus carolinensis*), and tree swallows (*Tachycineta bicolor*), as well as bluebirds, have used our milk cartons and plastic jugs, we have never had a house sparrow take one. They apparently are not suitable for house sparrows.

Unfortunately, bluebirds do not seem to be very enthusiastic about milk cartons and jugs either. Although they readily take to them in some areas, they shun them in others, and we suspect that they would always prefer a wooden box. We have also tried the two-liter plastic soda bottles and the gallon plastic milk jugs. Bluebirds show less interest in these than our paper cartons and the sturdier gallon jugs; thus, plastic and paper do not seem to be the answer to the house sparrow problem. Boxes of such materials are cost free and easy to make, however, and some people may find them worth a try.

Scriven (1989; 1993) says milk cartons and plastic jugs should never be used because they get so hot they can kill young birds. Milk cartons do not get hot, however, and neither do plastic jugs if they are properly ventilated. We have raised hundreds of bluebirds in these containers without ever losing any to heat stress. Most small birds maintain a body temperature of about 104 degrees Fahrenheit, thus are much more heat tolerant than we are. Although we have never lost young bluebirds to heat in jugs, we have seen them under stress in extreme weather. For this reason I usually try to place jugs in the partial shade of a tree in a fence row whenever one is available. Paper milk cartons do not present a heating problem.

Polyvinyl chloride (PVC) sewer pipe can be used to make a good bird house. Either four-inch or six-inch pipe can be used. Steve Gilbertson has designed an excellent sparrow-inhibiting box using four-inch pipe (see chapter 11).

Research at the University of Kentucky has shown that bluebirds prefer a box with a slot entrance to the standard circular entrance (McComb et al. 1987) and that house sparrows have a strong preference for the circular entrance (Davis 1989b). A slot entrance box with a standard depth of about five inches from the entrance to the floor is more likely to attract bluebirds than house sparrows. House

A standard slot entrance box

sparrows will take some of these boxes, however, and will occasionally evict bluebirds in order to obtain a nesting site. House sparrows
will fill the box with trash—grass, plastic, feathers, etc.—and make a
tunnel from the entrance to the floor. They lay their eggs almost on
the floor, as far from the entrance as they can get.

The more shallow the box, the less attractive it is to house sparrows. Therefore, where sparrows are a problem, we recommend that
the boxes be built with a slot entrance and no deeper than five inches.
Bluebirds will readily use boxes that are four inches deep. If sparrows
take a box, remove the nest and place a piece of wood on the floor to
make it more shallow. Continue until the sparrow abandons. Bluebirds will nest in a box as shallow as three inches, but they prefer it
deeper.

Zeleny (1976) recommends a depth of at least six inches. He says
that starlings will often disrupt a nest by reaching through the opening and that if they can reach far enough they may break the eggs, kill
the nestlings, or even kill an incubating bluebird. He recommends a
box deep enough that starlings cannot reach the bluebird nest.

A box with a circular entrance

We have no evidence, however, of starlings causing problems in our shallow boxes. Although they often try to gain entrance, they do not harm the bluebird nests within. In fact, even in boxes that for experimental purposes we made accessible to starlings, the starlings rarely bothered nesting bluebirds (Davis and McComb 1989), much to our surprise. We think that the effect of inhibiting house sparrows far outweighs the threat of starling interference, and we recommend a rather shallow box.

Bluebirds will use boxes with a wide variety of floor dimensions. We have had them nesting in boxes that were 3 x 3, 4 x 4, 5 x 5, and 6 x 6 inches. The first is too small and results in unnecessary crowding, and the last is obviously larger than needed. Bluebirders debate the relative merits of four- and five-square-inch floors, with advocates of the latter praising the ample room for a large growing brood. Floors should not be larger than five inches. Lumsden (1986) showed that bluebirds prefer a 4 x 4 floor to one 6 x 6 inches. After raising bluebirds in various boxes, I have decided that a floor 4 x 4 inches provides plenty of room and that there is no advantage to larger dimensions. A piece of two-by-four cut to a length of four inches provides an adequate floor whose actual dimensions are 3½ x 4 inches. Pitts (1988) tested floor sizes of 3 x 4 inches compared with those 4 x 5½ inches and found that bluebirds showed no preference. Clutch size, hatching, and fledging success were the same. Barber (1990) fledged seven bluebirds from one nesting in a box with a floor 4 x 4 inches and six from a box with a floor 3½ x 3½ inches. Nevertheless, many bluebirders prefer to make boxes with floor dimensions between four inches and five inches to allow for greater comfort for a large brood.

A variety of materials, from wood scraps to PVC pipe and plastic jugs, can be used to make nesting structures.

3
Choosing Sites

THE CHOICE OF SITES depends upon your circumstances. If you are developing a bluebird trail along a highway, at a state park, a military installation, or a ranch, you can be pretty particular about choosing ideal sites for your boxes. If you have a country home with a few acres or less, however, your choice of sites will be restricted. In any case, *sites* must be plural; you should either put up two or more boxes or have a second box ready to put up as needed.

The worst thing that can happen is to have a pair of bluebirds nesting in your box and have it taken over by house sparrows, which will build a nest over the eggs or young of the bluebirds. The bluebirds will abandon the site and may not come back even if you destroy the house sparrows and remove their nest. The evicted bluebirds will, however, readily move into another box in the vicinity if one is available. Their setback will be minor, and they will proceed with their new nest unmolested by the house sparrows.

If you are in the northern states, where tree swallows (*Tachycineta bicolor*) are common, you should erect two boxes at the same site. They can even be on the same post. Tree swallows will use one and bluebirds will use the other in peaceful coexistence. If only a single box is available, the birds will fight over it. Some people have recommended that paired boxes be about twenty-five feet apart, but Dorber (1988) found that when they were more than five feet apart, both boxes were likely to be taken by swallows.

Choose a site in the open away from woods or brush to avoid problems with rat snakes and house wrens. Black rat snakes (*Elaphe obsoleta*), which range throughout the eastern states except the northernmost regions, are one of the most common predators at the bluebird nest. In boxes placed at the forest edge, expect about half the

A house wren

bluebird nestings to be raided by snakes. Although the snakes will range out into the fields a hundred yards or more at night seeking prey, the probability of their finding the bluebird nest decreases with its distance from the woods (Davis and McComb 1988).

House wrens *(Troglodytes aedon)* can be a serious problem throughout their breeding range, in the northern half of the eastern states and into Canada. They often destroy bluebird nests, eggs, and even hatchlings, and will take over all the boxes in the vicinity. They forage on the ground, however, where they need the cover of woods or brush. Although they do not like to range out into the open they will occasionally fill boxes with their stick nests a hundred yards or more from any cover. The farther from trees or brush, the less likely your boxes will be taken by wrens.

Hill or valley makes no difference as a site. If the site is open grassland or scattered weeds, bluebirds will likely use it whether it is upland or lowland. Pastureland makes an excellent site.

The first choice is to wire the box to a steel post or to a woven wire fence. Avoid any post or fence with vines on it. The box should be on the side away from the livestock. If the fence has cattle on both sides, it can be used if the posts are tall enough that the animals cannot reach the box to rub their sides against it. Cattle will scratch themselves on a box until they destroy it or knock it down. Tuttle (1982) designed a guard for mounting boxes out in the pasture. See chapter 11.

If horses are in a field, a box must be placed not only on the side away from the animals but must be placed where they cannot reach it. Unless there is a barbed wire strand along the top of the fence, horses will reach over it and chew on the lid of the box. On wooden horse-farm fences we place boxes on the outside of the fence and low enough that the horses cannot reach them. Bluebirds will readily use a box only two or three feet above the ground. Of course, such a site is more susceptible to predation by house cats and raccoons.

Horses will chew the lids of boxes.

*Box mounted on
a tree trunk*

A steel post is somewhat preferable to a wooden one. House cats, like all animals, are lazy, and although they can easily jump to a box on a steel post they are more likely to climb the wooden post. Raccoons will readily climb any fence.

Utility poles make excellent sites for boxes. In a pasture field a box can be put on a utility pole about five feet above the ground where cattle cannot rub it off. Of course, one needs to get permission from the power company or telephone company to use their poles. They usually will not want a box nailed to a pole because it interferes with the lineman's need to climb the pole; however, arrangements can be made to erect boxes that will not interfere. Bird bander Ralph Bell of Clarksville, Pennsylvania, puts all his boxes on power poles with permission of the power company. See chapter 11 for Bell's method of attaching boxes to poles.

A tree trunk is a less desirable site. Bluebirds show a definite preference for boxes on posts or utility poles (Keegan 1988; Davis 1989c). Apparently, tree cavities belong to the starlings. Bluebirds and house sparrows almost never use tree cavities where starlings are present, and this appears to affect their interest in a box on a tree. In northwestern Minnesota, where starlings are not a factor, bluebirds readily use boxes on trees, whereas in Kentucky such sites are only occasionally used. A box on a tree is much more likely to be disturbed by squirrels. A circular entrance box is preferable to the slot entrance for boxes to be placed on trees. The slightest chewing on the entrance will make a slot box accessible to starlings, whereas a squirrel must do a lot more work on the round hole before starlings can get in.

If boxes must be placed on trees, choose trees with the longest expanse of bare trunk. It must be free of branches in the vicinity of the box.

Height above Ground

Bluebirds will readily nest at sites ranging from two feet to twenty feet or more above ground. Your usual choice of a site, however, should be about four or five feet above ground, about the height of a fence post. Higher sites should usually be avoided for two reasons. The higher the box, the more attractive it is to house sparrows. Also, boxes should usually be placed where it is most convenient to get to them to check them for problems with ants, wasps, mice, and house sparrows and to clean them out when necessary. Unfortunately, in some good bluebird habitats, such as public parklands, it may be necessary to place some or all of your boxes high to prevent vandalism. Boxes in such places sometimes have to be placed ten feet or so above ground, out of reach of a person with a baseball bat.

If house sparrows are a special problem, you may want to try placing boxes two or three feet above ground. The lower the box, the less interesting it will be to house sparrows; however, this idea must be balanced against other potential problems. Predators, especially house cats and raccoons, are more likely to find and raid boxes that are especially close to the ground.

Distance between Boxes

Since bluebirds are strongly territorial, no more than one box ordinarily will be used in one territory. If house sparrows are a problem, however, you may want to have more than one box within a territory. If house sparrows evict a pair of bluebirds they will readily move into the next empty box.

The size of a territory is variable and undefined, and depends somewhat on the individual bluebirds. Some individuals are more aggressive than others. One tenth of a mile (175 yards) is usually an adequate distance. If sites are separated by trees, a hill, a cliff, or a building, they can be placed closer. Some people have had general success with sites one hundred yards apart. We have heard of bluebirds nesting in two boxes only twenty-five feet apart, and there is a report of two instances of bluebirds nesting in both boxes where two were placed back to back on the same post (Dupree and Wright 1990). Such instances probably involve a single territory used by one male and two females.

If you have a trail with boxes on fences along a road, you may want to place them farther apart than necessary to separate territories. If boxes are less than about three hundred yards apart, a single raccoon may run your trail and raid as many as half a dozen consecutive boxes. Placing boxes two tenths of a mile apart will usually lessen this problem.

Direction the Box Should Face

Bluebirds do not seem to care which direction a box faces. You might want to face it away from the prevailing storms. Some people recommend facing the box east or northeast to avoid the hot afternoon sun. Another consideration is to try to face a box toward a tree within fifty yards or so, providing a refuge for the young bluebirds when they take their first flight from the box.

4

When to Erect Boxes

WHEN SHOULD YOU put up bluebird houses? Whenever you buy them or build them. They will not attract bluebirds if they are stored in your garage.

The generally recommended time is in late winter just before the bluebirds return from their winter home. Bluebirds are among our earliest migrants. Some are seeking nest sites in Kentucky in early March; in the northern states and Canada it may be a month later. You will have the largest percentage of your boxes used if you have them in place when the bluebirds arrive.

Boxes erected later in the season, however, will often be used. We have had reasonable success in Kentucky with boxes that we put up in May and June and even an occasional nesting in boxes placed in July. We have even had boxes get their first nesting in early August. You might as well put up the boxes and see what happens.

There are several sources of bluebirds that will use boxes that have been put up late. In good bluebird habitat there will be birds without nest sites if they must depend upon natural cavities. A pair of birds will commonly hang around a good territory all season without breeding. A box provided for such a pair in summer is likely to be occupied immediately and have a completed nest with eggs within a week. Early season explorers, on the other hand, are likely to wait a month or more before actually starting a family.

"Floaters" are another source of bluebirds for late boxes. These are birds without territories or nest sites, and they wander throughout the breeding season. Birds that have had a disaster at an earlier nesting attempt may also use late boxes. If bluebirds are evicted by house sparrows, house wrens, or ants, or if their nests have been raided by cats or raccoons, they will not go back to the box but will seek a

*Removing
a house
sparrow
nest*

new site. Occasionally a box or natural nest cavity is destroyed and the birds using it must seek a new site. Boxes can be erected in areas where no bluebirds are to be seen, yet bluebirds will appear one day and move in.

Autumn is an ideal time to put up boxes. Beautiful weather can make for pleasant work in contrast to the cold, wind, rain, and snow often encountered in late winter and early spring. If you live within the winter range of bluebirds, erecting boxes in the fall has the added advantage of providing shelter for the birds on cold winter nights. In my numerous experiments with nest box designs, I have usually laid out my plans and put up my boxes in the fall. Of course, boxes placed in the fall need to be checked just before the summer resident bluebirds start to arrive. Checking boxes and cleaning out an occasional mouse nest is a nicer job than working with pliers, wire, hammer, and cold fingers in February.

I had always thought that our winter bluebirds in Kentucky were migrants from northern states and our summer resident birds would all migrate. Tuttle (1987b), however, found with his banded birds that some raised in his boxes in central Ohio used the boxes in winter. Thus another reason for erecting boxes in autumn is that some of your winter resident bluebirds may claim them as nest sites.

5
Through the Seasons

I F Y O U L I V E from the Ohio River Valley southward or in the coastal states as far north as Connecticut, bluebirds will be with you throughout the winter. Although some of these birds may be migrants from farther north with no intention of nesting, they will appreciate the protection of your boxes as roosting sites on cold winter nights. Even as far north as Michigan some bluebirds are permanent residents and use the boxes in winter (Pinkowski 1974, 1977a). Some people plug the ventilation holes in autumn to provide their bluebirds with a snug winter home. Tuttle (1987b) found higher survival in his winterized boxes and kept his weatherstripping on through the spring when young bluebirds are subject to cold stress.

Older males arrive on the breeding grounds an average of a month earlier than the yearlings, and they immediately establish territories. An old male can reclaim an area used the previous year by driving off a male that had arrived earlier. Some yearling males do not establish territory and breed (Pinkowski 1977a).

The first arrivals appear about a month before serious nesting starts. When a pair of bluebirds discovers a box, the male goes in and out repeatedly, fluttering his wings as if to tell his mate that he has found a suitable site. Both birds then thoroughly inspect their prospective new home, after which they may remain in the vicinity or they may disappear for a few weeks. If the box is checked, it is likely to be empty or likely to contain a tiny trace of nesting material: one or two fragments of dried grass about the size of a thread and usually not more than about three inches long. This trace of material, easily overlooked, means that the box has been staked out by a pair of bluebirds and that eventually they will build a nest there.

The earliest birds that have found a nest site are in no hurry to

A house wren has taken this box.

begin building. Cold wet weather is likely to prevail for some time, and there is no advantage to starting too early. Insects are scarce in spring and growing youngsters put a heavy demand on the parents' ability to provide food. A few cool days when the young are near fledging sometimes leads to starvation of the first brood, a problem never encountered later in the season when grasshoppers and caterpillars become abundant.

Between the time when the birds arrive and the time at which nesting begins all bluebirds that have not found a site are foraging over the countryside looking for suitable places. Boxes erected during this period are likely to attract tenants.

If a box is erected or discovered after serious nesting time has arrived, the bluebirds are likely to get started with housekeeping right away. Morgan Yewell put up a box one morning in April in Kentucky, saw a bluebird on it at noon, and found a complete nest when he checked it twenty-six hours after he had put it up.

There is considerable variation among individuals in the time they start nesting. Some will complete the nest in early April, while others will not start nesting until well into May. This, of course, varies geographically; in northern Minnesota nesting does not begin until May, whereas in parts of Texas it begins in February.

Some birds put a trace of dry grass in a box as soon as they find it and do no construction for several weeks. Others will start a nest, leave it for several weeks, and then finish it and lay eggs. Still others will complete a nest and leave it for weeks before laying eggs. Four or five weeks is not at all unusual between the time a pair of bluebirds takes a box and the time of egg laying. We once had a pair build a nest in April but lay their first eggs and raise a brood in July.

Only rarely will bluebirds abandon a box for no apparent cause. In such cases, one of the pair may have been killed or the pair may have found a better site. Nest abandonment for cause, however, is common, and since bluebirds are very tolerant of human disturbance at the box, your checking on them as frequently as once a day is in their best interest. Ants may invade the nest, where they will be inconspicuous and harmless while their population builds up. Eventually they will cause the birds to desert the nest. If, however, the ants are found early and destroyed, the bluebirds will remain.

The nest is usually constructed of dry grass. Where pine trees occur nearby the nest may be made of dry pine needles, and in areas where crown vetch (*Coronilla varia*) covers highway cuts or other reclaimed land the dead stems of this vine are used. In any case, the bluebird nest is nearly always constructed entirely of the same material. In rare instances one or two small feathers may be incorporated into the nests, and occasionally horse hair is used.

The new nest is a neat cup. Sometimes when checking an unoccupied nest you will find that the surface has been messed and is no longer smooth. What causes this is unknown, but it always means abandonment. Such a nest should be removed; bluebirds will not nest in the box unless the messed nest is removed. When the nest is removed, however, they will nearly always start again.

A bluebird nest

Bluebirds sometimes abandon a nest with eggs. A late snow will cause the birds to abandon. Several days of cool rainy weather will also cause the clutch to be abandoned. Abandoned eggs tend to work down into the nest. They have nest material beside them and sometimes even on top of them. An active clutch always sits atop a neat cup of a nest. Abandoned nest and eggs should probably be removed when recognized; however, it is routine for birds that abandon an early clutch because of bad weather to build a new nest over the abandoned eggs.

The first clutch of the season is most commonly five eggs, with four being the number next frequent. Incubation begins after the clutch is complete so that all young hatch at the same time. The incubation period is about fourteen days. Incubation is irregular, and the female often leaves the nest. She spends less time on the eggs during warm days than during cool weather. Eggs in an active nest are usually warm to the touch. Bluebird eggs are easily recognized by their pale blue color (occasionally pure white) and size, about 21 mm long.

Behavior of adults at the nest varies among individuals. Some females take flight as a person approaches the box, whereas others

Young bluebirds in the nest

will sit quietly on the nest while the box is opened for inspection. Most males remain close by during incubation, often perching on the fence beside the box. Other males are seldom seen near the box. Some pairs seem exceptionally shy; even when feeding the young they make a quick visit to the box and vanish to a distant feeding ground. Others are usually visible, doing most of their feeding within sight of the box. A common pattern when there are young in the box is for both parents to sit quietly on an overhead wire while the nest is being inspected. Even when it is necessary to remove a colony of ants, build a new nest, or even move the box, the parents usually watch quietly and readily resume housekeeping chores once the intruder has left. Only occasional individuals are aggressive; some parents will dive toward the intruder, especially when the young are near fledging.

When the eggs hatch, the tiny, wet, and nearly naked young are blind and helpless. At this time the female broods them almost constantly, spending more time at the nest than during incubation. She sits especially close during the cool weather with her first brood of the spring. As soon as the newly hatched young are dry, they are ready to be fed. The male brings tiny insects to the young, which raise their heads and open their mouths in response to any disturbance at the nest. Although the young grow rapidly, they remain blind until the eyes open about the sixth day. Pin feathers begin to show at about one week, and at two weeks the young are well feathered. The sex of the young can be recognized at this time; the males already have the brilliant blue of the wing feathers, whereas the females are more dull.

Caterpillars are the most common food item brought to the young, making up 32 percent of the items. Grasshoppers and crickets make up 26 percent, with spiders being the third most abundant item at 11 percent. A wide variety of insects and other invertebrates and occasional small fruit make up the remainder of the diet (Pinkowski 1978a).

Unlike house sparrows, robins, and many of our other small songbirds, young bluebirds do not leave the nest until they are well developed and quite able to fly. Their first flight is strong and may

Feeding

*Typical behavior
for bluebirds
near fledging*

cover fifty yards or so, usually carrying the young to a tree or other elevated perch site. Whereas many species of songbirds fledge at two weeks, young bluebirds usually remain in the box until nearly three weeks old.

When near fledging young bluebirds spend much of their time with one or more of the brood looking out the entrance, often with the head and shoulders protruding. At this time they should not be disturbed; they should be allowed to fledge naturally with the parents coaxing them out and being present to care for them. Until they are ready to fledge, however, the young are not likely to flee when you open the box to check on their welfare, which you should do at least once a week to see that there are no dead young and that the ants are not taking over. From the time the young first open their eyes until they are ready to fledge they will respond to your opening the box by scrunching down into the nest and away from the light. If you wish to remove a young bird for inspection you will find it not at all enthusiastic about the idea. The young become so tightly packed together that you will have difficulty getting your fingers between them, and once you do get hold of an individual it will hold tightly to nesting material with its toes. When necessary to remove the young because of an ant problem, simply remove the nest and place it in the shade. The young usually will scrunch down in the nest and remain quiet while you prepare the box for their return.

After the young leave the box, they usually leave the area. Sometime between ten days and a month or more, however, the parents usually will return to the box where they have been successful in raising a first brood and build a new nest. Although they will quite readily build a new nest over the old one, it is usually a good practice to remove the old nest when the young have fledged, because it is more attractive to ants than is an empty box. Also parasitic blow flies, the larvae of which feed on young birds, are likely to have pupated on the floor of the box and they can be removed and destroyed at this time. These parasites are usually of minor concern, for they are seldom numerous enough to harm the young birds. When you remove an old nest you should carry it off; if left at the site, its odor might attract predators.

The second nesting differs in some ways from the first. If there were five eggs in the first clutch there will more likely be four in the second. The problem of cold wet weather may be replaced with a problem of excessive heat. Even though bluebirds like a box out in full sunlight, mortality because of heat is uncommon.

Insects are much more abundant when the second brood is in the box, and starvation is almost never a problem. Even if something happens to one of the parents, the other one has no trouble providing enough food. Sometimes the young from the first brood will return to the vicinity of the nest site.

Altruism is not uncommon among bluebirds. Young from an earlier brood may help their parents feed a new brood, and a yearling male has been known to help his parents raise his new siblings (Pinkowski 1975). An adult male has been known to adopt a brood, helping a widowed female care for it (Pinkowski 1978b). Meek and Robertson (1992), however, found that most males that joined wid-

Mother and young

ows did not feed the young, and those that did fed less often than real fathers. A new female once moved in and incubated the eggs of one that had been killed by a cat (Hamilton 1943). In Alabama, one ambitious male bluebird helped raise four broods in one season, the broods belonging to two females (Tucker 1990). In Georgia, Casses (1992) watched in April as bluebirds built a nest in a box in her yard and one male and three adult females raised a brood of four, with all four adults feeding the young.

In the northernmost states and Canada, two annual broods is the usual pattern. In Kentucky, a third brood is common, occurring in about a third of our birds. In the Deep South, as many as four broods are raised in a season (Krueger 1991b). Clutch size decreases as the season progresses (Peakall 1970), and for the third brood, clutch size is usually three. This is strange, because in late summer food is most abundant, whereas first broods in spring often starve in the nest.

As the summer progresses, bluebirds become ever more conspicuous in areas where boxes have been provided. Family groups of five to seven birds are often seen along a fence or on overhead wires. Individuals make frequent flights to the ground to catch an insect and return to an elevated perch. Grasshoppers become abundant in late summer and the families of bluebirds feast and fatten in preparation for migration.

As compared to many of our songbirds, the migration of bluebirds is not very extensive; several hundred miles is usual. Those in the northernmost states and Canada move south to regions of milder winters. The winter range of the eastern bluebird is usually from the Ohio River Valley southward to the Gulf Coast and up the Atlantic Coast to Connecticut (Layton 1989).

In winter, bluebirds usually occur in small groups of half a dozen or so, perhaps family groups. Pinkowski (1974) observed a family group that remained together through the winter in Michigan. In the Deep South, flocks of up to a hundred are sometimes seen foraging in winter. In central Kentucky we have seen a flock of about seventy-five birds, but groups of less than a dozen are usual. In winter the bluebirds are often found in brushy areas and forest edge, habitats they do not favor at other seasons.

Winter is a crucial period for bluebirds. The weather is by far the most important factor in determining their population (Sauer and Droege 1990). The severe winter of 1976-77 nearly eliminated the eastern bluebird. In Kentucky, continuous snow cover broke all previous records by a substantial margin and the bitter cold and long-lasting snow cover extended into the Deep South. Few bluebirds survived to use nest boxes during the breeding season of 1977 (Pitts 1978a; 1978b).

During cold weather bluebirds roost in cavities, and providing roost sites can help them survive. Although special winter roost boxes have been designed, there is no evidence that they are ever used; an ordinary nest box is satisfactory. Providing winter roosts is a good reason to erect your nesting boxes in the fall. We once put up fifty boxes in central Kentucky in October for an experiment in nest box selection and inspected the boxes in late February. Eighteen of them had been used as winter roosts, evidenced by the bluebird feathers and accumulated droppings containing seeds of poke weed and hawthorn berries.

Sometimes half a dozen bluebirds or more will cluster in a box on a cold night to conserve heat. It is a good idea to plug ventilation holes for the winter to help the birds survive the cold spells. You might also leave old nests in place to provide insulation.

Toward the end of winter bluebirds begin their northward migration. They are among our earliest migrants and begin prospecting for nest sites as soon as they arrive. Here in central Kentucky, we try to have our boxes cleaned and repaired and ready for inspection by the first week in March.

As more people take to feeding bluebirds in winter, their survival during severe weather likely will be enhanced; perhaps we will not again experience the massive mortality of the winter of 1976-77. Although bluebirds will not eat bird seed and do not join other birds at the usual backyard feeder, there are many foods they will take when provided in special feeders they have been trained to use. Not only can you help them survive the winter, you can have them as regular guests at your feeder throughout the year.

___6___
Bluebirds at
Your Feeder

BLUEBIRDS DO NOT ORDINARILY come to a feeder. They are not seed eaters and are not attracted to the fare in the ordinary backyard bird feeder. Bluebirds are insectivorous when bugs are available. During winter, they eat various small fruit such as dogwood, rosehips, poke, honeysuckle, sumac, and hawthorn.

There are numerous things that are readily available to people that bluebirds will eat. This includes raisins, currants, or other dried fruit cut into small bits; shelled sunflower seed; peanut butter, peanut hearts, or peanut bits; chopped nuts; cornbread; suet; and mealworms. A mixture called miracle meal, developed by Carol Harmon, is popu-

Insects are the favorite meal of bluebirds.

lar with people who feed bluebirds. It is made by mixing three cups of yellow corn meal, one cup of flour, and half a pound of lard. Some people add peanut hearts or peanut butter; some use bacon grease or shortening. A commercial bluebird feed is available at all Wild Birds Unlimited stores.

Unfortunately, putting out suitable foods alone will not attract bluebirds. Many people feed suet and attract woodpeckers, nuthatches, titmice, and chickadees but never bluebirds. Bluebirds, for some strange reason, need to be taught to come to a feeder.

Teaching bluebirds to use a feeder is a rewarding experience. In regions where they are winter residents, feeding can be important to their survival. When snow and ice cover the natural food, bluebird mortality is high. Also, bluebirds must compete with the great flocks of starlings and robins, which move in and strip the trees and shrubs of berries. Availability of food in winter is now the major factor that limits the population of bluebirds.

Joe Huber in Ohio was one of the first people to be successful in providing winter food for bluebirds. He cut fruiting stems from multiflora rose and other wild roses and stored them in a shed. In winter he stuck the stems into holes he had drilled in a platform feeder in his yard and the bluebirds came to eat.

Most of the foods liked by bluebirds are also attractive to starlings. If you make miracle meal and put it on a platform feeder, the starlings and blue jays will clean it up before the bluebirds can find it. For this reason, bluebird feeders are built specially to exclude these other birds. Bluebird feeders are accessible only by one or more entrance holes 1½ inches in diameter. Such feeders can be purchased from Wild Birds Unlimited, or you can make your own. See chapter 11.

Teaching bluebirds to use a feeder sometimes requires considerable effort and patience. Tina and Curtis Dew (Dew et al. 1986) have been able to get bluebirds to use their feeders year round and have described their methods. The Dews report that bluebirds will learn to use a feeder sooner if it is put out in winter when insects and other natural foods are getting scarce and harder to find. They say that bluebirds can be taught to use a feeder at any season, however; it just takes longer in summer when food is abundant.

The Dews suggest that you start your training program with some natural foods. Pick bunches of ripe berries from such things as dogwood, holly, pokeweed, pyracantha, blueberries, or other fruit that grows naturally nearby. In Kentucky we have noticed that bluebirds feed the nestlings of their late broods extensively on wild cherry, which ripens in August. This might be a good fruit to try at that season.

The Dews recommend that you start with a flat board feeder mounted on a post near your house where you can watch the bluebirds. Your feeder will eventually be mounted upon this board. The board should be longer than your feeder, so that after the feeder is mounted the board extends several inches beyond each end, providing a platform beneath the entrance holes where the birds can stand before learning to use the entrances and where food can be placed when training your bluebirds.

Place the natural food on your feeding platform. It may take several days for the bluebirds to discover this potential feast. After they get used to the feeding platform, mount your feeder on it. Continue feeding at the ends of the platform and, of course, put various foods in the feeder. Place food near the entrance with some both inside and outside the feeder. Once the birds learn to go into the feeder, you can place all food inside.

Morris M. Green (1986) of Walkersville, Maryland, has been quite successful with winter feeders. He feeds miracle meal and suet ground like hamburger. He recommends building T-shaped perches out in front of the feeders. He drives a post in the ground fifteen to twenty feet in front of the feeder and nails to it a piece of wood eighteen inches long and about ½ x ½ inch. An ordinary small branch should do just as well. The bluebirds make heavy use of such a perch, nearly always alighting on it before and after visiting his feeder. The bluebirds use the perch all day; sometimes several are on it at one time.

One way to start artificial feeding of bluebirds if you have them nesting in a box in your yard is to place food on the roof. You can try fruit such as raisins cut in half (Harry Krueger has found that bluebirds take to raisins much more readily if they are dyed with red food coloring), or you can try mealworms, which are likely to be accepted right away. Mealworms should be placed in a shallow container such

*Young bluebird
on the roof*

as a jar lid. Test first to see that they cannot climb out, then place the container on the roof of the nesting box. After the birds learn to eat mealworms, you can place the container on the platform where you plan to build your feeder.

Mealworms are available at your pet store, but if you plan to feed many of them you may want to raise your own (Dupree 1988). Buy a bag of bran at your feed store and put it into covered containers such as five-gallon plastic pails. It will take several months before your colony gets going well enough to supply your bluebirds. Throw in an apple core or a slice of potato occasionally for moisture; if such is not available, the adults, which are dark beetles nearly an inch long, will eat the pupae.

Andrew Troyer has trained wild bluebirds to eat from his hand. He described his method at the Ohio Bluebird Society meeting held October 15, 1994.

Troyer raises mealworms, which he finds to be much more enticing to bluebirds than various fruits and berries. He mounted a wooden platform on a photographer's tripod so that it is easily movable and adjustable. The platform has sides nearly an inch high so that the mealworms cannot easily escape.

He put the feeder out near an active nest box, and the bluebirds became accustomed to using it. In gradual steps he moved it nearer his house until he finally had it just outside a window. With bluebirds using the feeder regularly, Troyer pulled down the window shade so that the birds could not see him and then put his hand with mealworms out the window and onto the feeder tray. After the birds accepted this, he gradually raised the shade until he was in full view.

The most difficult step was going outside; the birds shied away from him. He overcame this by partially shielding himself behind a lawn chair. The birds finally came to accept him completely. He now can step outdoors and whistle his feeding signal, and the bluebirds will come in from all directions. The birds are so accustomed to this system that they will feed from the hand of a stranger.

Troyer has published a colorful booklet describing how you too can get bluebirds to feed from your hand. See the Appendix for his address.

An important adjunct to a feeder is a bird bath. Get a lightweight one that you can easily handle and keep clean, not one of those concrete monstrosities. Have a heater for winter, and keep the bath filled and clean. Bluebirds are very particular about having their bath water clean. They really love a bird bath and will use it every day, even during the coldest winter.

The Dews (Dew et al. 1986) have bluebirds taking food from their feeder to young in the nest. After the young fledge, the whole family comes in and the young learn to use the feeder. One might be concerned that the birds might become too dependent and not learn to forage on their own; however, the Dews report that even with their favorite food of chopped raisins, the bluebirds only supplement their diet at the feeder and spend plenty of time catching insects.

One of the problems with a bluebird feeder is that the first time a bird uses it, the bird may have trouble finding the exit and may insist on trying to get out through the glass. This is especially common with young birds on their first visit. You can help alleviate this problem by putting an entrance low near the floor where it is more easily found. You can even make several entrances and put entrances on both ends of your feeder. An idea that some people have tried and claim success for is to run strips of black tape across the glass in a checkerboard fashion.

Several studies have shown that weather is by far the most important factor limiting bluebird populations, with severe winters causing heavy mortality (Sauer and Droege 1990). If you live in the winter range of the eastern bluebird, roughly the Ohio River Valley southward, your feeding program can be critical to their survival.

7
Guests and Pests

I F Y O U H A V E the proper kind of boxes in good locations you
will probably attract more bluebirds than any other creature. However, your box provides excellent shelter—a quality that may be scarce
in the areas you have chosen—and many types of animals are potential tenants. Some are delightful guests that we are glad to have, others are interesting but may sometimes be pests, and a few may cause
serious problems. If you have an extensive bluebird trail and run it
for several years you will have the opportunity to see many interesting creatures. The following are some of your most likely guests.

Tree Swallow *(Tachycineta bicolor)*

This elegant bird, with its graceful flight, flashing its brilliant green
back and pure white underparts, is one of our more desirable cavity-
nesting birds. A northern species, it has been extending its range southward, perhaps as a result of extensive bluebird nest box projects. It
now nests regularly in Kentucky, although it is still uncommon and
we are always delighted to have tree swallows use one of our boxes.
In the northernmost states and Canada, however, tree swallows are
so abundant that they usually will occupy more of your boxes than
the bluebirds will, and the two species often fight over the nest sites.
They may destroy each other's eggs and evict each other several times
during a season, thus causing problems for both species (Tuttle 1987a).
In some areas, tree swallows take so many of the boxes that bluebirders despair that there will be enough sites available for their favor-
ites. Fortunately, this problem has been solved in recent years by a
process known as pairing of boxes. Where tree swallows are common, you may erect two boxes at the same site. They can be a few feet

apart, or they may even be mounted on the same pole. Bluebirds will use one and tree swallows the other. Dorber (1988) recommends the boxes be no more than five feet apart; otherwise swallows may take both. Although both species are territorial, territorial birds usually defend an area only against their own species. If bluebirds and tree swallows are not competing for the same nest box, they get along fine. Rendell and Robertson (1990) found that, given a choice, tree swallows tend to choose boxes farther away from the forest edge than do bluebirds. Tree swallows have a strong affinity for water; boxes in upland sites away from ponds and lakes are less likely to be taken by swallows.

Tuttle (1991) has recently done an analysis of data from his studies in Delaware State Park, Ohio, where bluebirds and tree swallows both began nesting as a result of boxes being placed for them. Both species have increased over the years since he began in 1977. Tuttle's conclusion was that, in spite of the competition, the tree swallows actually helped the bluebirds. House wrens were a major enemy of bluebirds, and tree swallows drove off wrens, defending not only their own boxes but also the ones occupied by the bluebirds.

Don Wilkins in northern Minnesota does not pair his boxes. He is interested in attracting bluebirds and believes that pairing is a waste of boxes. By carefully selecting his sites, he has been able to get bluebirds in nearly every box. He says the important factor is to have the boxes ready early so that nesting by bluebirds is well underway by the time the swallows are interested. Wilkins says the swallows wait peacefully until the bluebirds fledge, then move in and raise their broods. He took me to a series of boxes he had on power poles. At several of these there were pairs of swallows sitting quietly on the wires above the boxes where bluebirds incubated. Perhaps the fact that Wilkins has nearly all his boxes on utility poles is important. Gillis (1989) found that bluebirds can defend their boxes from swallows if they have an overhead perch but cannot defend if the box is on a fence. I saw only one of Wilkins's boxes that was occupied by swallows, and it was on a fence.

Tree swallow nests are easily recognized. They are so heavily lined with feathers that they look like a feather duster. House sparrow nests often contain lots of feathers, but they are also lined with various other materials such as plastic and grass. Tree swallow eggs are also distinctive. They are slimmer than bluebird eggs and pure white (bluebirds occasionally lay white eggs).

Usually when tree swallows discover a person in the vicinity of their box, both birds will fly overhead objecting to the intrusion. If the female is incubating, however, she will usually sit tight while you open and close the box.

Violet-green Swallow *(Tachycincta thalassina)*

The range of this common western swallow overlaps that of the tree swallow and the western and mountain bluebirds. Similar to the tree swallow, with nest and eggs almost identical, this little swallow is a serious threat to the western bluebird and often takes over its nest sites. Some people have had success with groups of three boxes at a site, one taken by tree swallows, one by violet-green swallows and one by bluebirds. Prescott and Gillis (1985), however, had their best success in dealing with swallow competition when they placed two boxes on opposite sides of a tree trunk.

Chickadee *(Parus* sp.)

One of the several species of chickadees is found nearly everywhere in the U.S. The Carolina chickadee *(Parus carolinensis)* is common throughout most of the eastern states. Chickadees frequently nest in bluebird boxes. They are usually woodland birds and are more likely to take boxes in or near the woods. A box near a patch of trees too young to provide natural cavities is especially likely to attract chickadees. Chickadees are delightful birds and no one should object to having them take a box that was meant for bluebirds. Chickadees start nesting even earlier than most of the bluebirds, and boxes frequently raise both species; bluebirds do not hesitate to build a nest on top of the old chickadee nest. Unfortunately, bluebirds do not always wait for the chickadees to finish with their nesting. Reed (1989) watched bluebirds remove the nest and eggs of chickadees from a box. The gentle little chickadee is at the bottom of pecking order among cavity-nesting birds. Some trail monitors protect their chickadees from bluebirds by adding a hole restricter, a piece of wood or plastic with a hole only an inch or an inch and a quarter in diameter, when they find an active chickadee nest. Chickadees raise a single large brood, usually six or seven offspring. If their first or second efforts are unsuccessful, they will keep trying: thus it is not unusual to have chickadees move into a box as late as May or June.

In Kentucky we have been surprised to find chickadees using boxes placed in the open as far as a quarter of a mile from any woodland. The least bit of scattered shrubbery or occasional tree seems to provide adequate habitat for these sprites. Nearly all the boxes that we place appear to be susceptible to use by chickadees.

Our chickadee nests are made entirely of green moss and lined with soft fur. Until the large brood of youngsters broaden it, the nest cup is only about two inches wide. The tiny pink eggs, speckled with brown, are only about 14 mm long.

Tufted Titmouse *(Parus bicolor)*

Very common in the Southeast (with related species in the Southwest), this species becomes scarce to absent in the northern states. Although titmice will nest in bird houses, they are encountered less frequently than chickadees. These pleasant little birds are a welcome addition to the bluebird trail. Like chickadees, titmice are woodland birds; we have, however, had them nesting in our bluebird boxes placed on fences out in the open on Kentucky horse farms.

The titmouse nest is made of leaves, bark, grass, roots, and green moss, and is lined with soft fur. The chamber is larger than that of a chickadee, about three inches across. The brown-speckled white eggs are similar to those of a chickadee but larger, about 20 mm long.

Like chickadees and bluebirds and in contrast to house sparrows, young titmice stay in the box until they are remarkably mature, strong fliers with a tail half the length of that of the adult.

House Wren *(Troglodytes aedon)*

With a breeding range throughout the northern states and southern Canada southward into Kentucky, the house wren is one of the birds most easily attracted to an artificial nest box. To folks living in the cities and suburbs, the tiny wren with its bubbling song is a delightful sprite, and neighbors compete with one another to get the territorial wrens to nest in a box in the backyard. The tiny creatures can enter a hole as small as three quarters of an inch in diameter. (An easy way to make a good wren house is to draw a circle around a quarter on a dry gourd and cut out the hole with a knife.)

Though house wrens are welcome in the city, they can be a major problem on the bluebird trail. For bluebirds in some northern states, house wrens are the most common problem. Many otherwise good sites for bluebirds have to be passed over when erecting boxes because of the house wren problem.

Fortunately, house wrens arrive at the nesting grounds four to six weeks after the bluebirds, so many bluebirds can get an early brood

A house wren inspects a box.

Bluebird eggs destroyed by a house wren.

raised before the house wrens are ready to cause trouble. In our experience, the wrens do not bother bluebirds if the young are more than a week old; they wait until the bluebirds fledge, then build atop the old nest. Wrens raise two broods in a season and are a threat to the second and third nestings of bluebirds (Tuttle 1991).

If a bluebird nest is at an earlier stage, however, the wren simply takes over. Each egg receives a single puncture hole from the beak. They are occasionally shattered and are often removed by the wren and dropped on the ground. Joe Huber (1992) watched a house wren carry a bluebird egg from a box at his home and drop the egg on his lawn. He found all four of the bluebird eggs scattered on the lawn. Hatchling bluebirds are simply thrown out to perish on the ground. Sometimes the wrens will remove the bluebird nest, but most often they simply build their nest upon it.

A house wren nest is distinctive. It consists of dry sticks; no other creature puts sticks in a bird house. A completed wren nest does not look like a nest at all. It appears as if the box is completely filled with sticks and the entrance blocked; however, there will be a tiny passage leading back and down to the nest chamber. The chamber itself is lined with horse hair, soft shredded dry bark, feathers, or other material providing a fairly soft lining to the pile of sticks. The chamber is only about two inches wide. The tiny pink eggs, heavily speckled with small flecks of brown, usually number from five to eight.

The house wren problem cannot be solved by pairing boxes, the method that has been so successful in dealing with tree swallows. The male house wren will simply fill any and all boxes in the vicinity with sticks. This tendency to build dummy nests is one of the least desirable characteristics of house wrens. With all available boxes filled with these dummy nests, they cannot be used by other birds, and yet the wrens will only complete the chamber in only one box. Many blue-

A house wren's nest

birds are prevented from raising a second brood because the box is full of sticks. If the sticks are removed, they are likely to be replaced.

House wrens forage on the ground and must have some cover. They like woods, shrubs, brush, hedges, and fence rows. They never forage out in the open pasture. Thus you can avoid a wren problem by placing your boxes away from cover; the farther away the less likely they are to be visited by wrens. Wrens seldom nest in a box one hundred yards or more from cover, although they will often wander out and place a few sticks and occasionally build a dummy nest in such boxes.

House wrens are native migratory birds and are protected by federal law. It is illegal to destroy their nests, eggs, or young. Thus you should allow them to use your bluebird boxes when they take over. When some sticks appear in a box well out into a pasture, however, I usually remove them. Such dummy nests would never be used by the wrens, and the farther away from cover the boxes are, the less likely that the wrens will replace the sticks. Thus removing the sticks simply makes the box available for bluebirds.

Richard Tuttle, who found that half his chickadee nests were being destroyed by house wrens, has been testing a new idea that he thinks may also work to protect bluebird nests. After his chickadees have laid eggs, he attaches a piece of wood to the front of the roof so that it comes down just far enough to obstruct a view of the entrance. A space between this board and the entrance of about an inch and a half allows room for the chickadee to go up under and into the entrance. The wren does not see an entrance and we hope he is not likely to investigate the box.

In the vicinity of Lexington, Kentucky, house wrens have increased dramatically in recent years, perhaps as a result of our erecting bluebird boxes. The wrens have extended their occupancy into more open areas, using boxes in habitat that does not look suitable for wrens and appropriating more and more of our bluebird boxes. Perhaps our raising wrens is rendering more areas unsuitable for bluebirds. Because of this potential problem some trail monitors do not let wrens nest in their boxes; they remove each pile of sticks that appears before the wrens get a chance to complete a nest.

Carolina Wren *(Thryothorus ludovicianus)*

This wren is common throughout the southeastern United States. The Carolina wren usually prefers a cavity more open than a box for its nest. A flower pot on a shelf in the shed, a rafter of an outbuilding, a can on its side in the garage, or a hanging flower basket on the patio provide likely sites for this large wren with the loud pleasant song.

In recent years we have had several Carolina wrens nest in our boxes. We suspect that they find our slot entrance and rather shallow boxes more satisfactory than the old-style bird houses.

The Carolina wren constructs a nest of dry leaves interwoven with roots, dry grass, and bark. The chamber is usually lined with strips of bark from grapevines, with perhaps a few feathers and even some plastic. The nest is partially arched over from behind, making it clearly visible through the entrance of a slot box, somewhat similar to the nests of mice and house sparrows. It can be distinguished from these in that the wren nest is mainly of leaves, whereas the sparrow's is mainly grass, and the mouse covers the chamber entirely with a soft fluffy material.

The Carolina wren, of course, is an honorable citizen and a desirable addition to the menagerie that you might find if you run an extensive bluebird trail.

Brown-headed Nuthatch *(Sitta pusilla)*

People who live in the Deep South are sometimes honored to have this acrobatic little fellow nest in their bluebird boxes. The nests are said to be constructed of grass, cotton, pieces of pine needles, wool, and feathers. There is one record of this nuthatch destroying the eggs of a bluebird (Hartley 1989) There is also a record of one helping to feed bluebird nestings (Stroud 1990).

White-breasted Nuthatch *(Sitta carolinensis)*

A woodland species generally distributed across the nation, this nuthatch is not usually attracted to bluebird houses. We have only seen it nesting once, in a box placed in the edge of the woods.

Ash-throated Flycatcher *(Myiarchus cinerascens)*

This desirable citizen of the southwestern and Pacific coast states will often nest in bluebird boxes that are in or near woods, scattered trees, or brush. The nest is constructed of grass, weed stems, rootlets, and sometimes bits of dried manure and is lined with hair and fur.

Great Crested Flycatcher *(Myiarchus cinerascens)*

A bird of the woodlands, this resident of the eastern states will nest in bird houses; however, it is usually too large to get into a bluebird box unless the entrance has been enlarged by rodents or woodpeckers. The nest is made of leaves, twigs, hair, feathers, bark fibers, rope, and plastic, and nearly always includes a snake skin.

House Sparrow *(Passer domesticus)*

The bane of bluebirds and bluebirders everywhere, the European house sparrow, introduced to North America in 1850, takes over many nest sites provided for bluebirds and is apparently the sole reason that bluebirds are almost never found nesting in the suitable habitat provided by our cities and suburbs. House sparrows will expel blue-birds, destroy eggs and young, and even kill adult bluebirds, although Gowaty (1981) found that the farther along the bluebirds are in the breeding cycle the less likely that they will be evicted; house spar-rows will usually chose an empty box rather than evict bluebirds.

The male house sparrow fills the box with nesting material, mostly dry grass but with a generous helping of feathers, plastic, ciga-rette filters, and other trash. The nest is a bulky, trashy mess in con-trast to the neat cup of the bluebird. In the earliest stage of nest build-ing, which involves only dry grass, sometimes one cannot tell whether the nest belongs to a house sparrow or a bluebird, although the spar-row usually uses slightly coarser material and sometimes includes roots and seed heads and a sprig of green vegetation. As the male house sparrow builds his nest, he spends many hours in the box, on the box, and perched beside the box. He chirps repeatedly to attract a mate, and if he does not succeed he may continue throughout the

A starling trying to enter a box

summer unless he is trapped and destroyed or the box is removed or made unsuitable for sparrows. For solutions to the house sparrow problem, see chapter 8, Foiling House Sparrows.

European Starling *(Sturnus vulgaris)*

This ubiquitous pest was introduced to North America in 1890. Like the house sparrow, this nonnative species is not protected by law. The starling has spread across the continent, and today it owns the natural tree cavities in the cities and farms; neither bluebirds nor house sparrows use natural cavities in living trees where starlings are found today.

Fortunately, starlings can be excluded from a bluebird house because they are bigger than bluebirds. An inch and a half circular hole or a slot entrance no wider that 30 mm will exclude starlings.

Occasionally a squirrel will enlarge an entrance and admit starlings. When this happens, the starlings should be evicted and the box should be replaced or repaired.

Starlings build a shallow nest of coarse straw and leaves. The eggs, usually four or five, are a light blue, paler than those of robins and bluebirds, and at about 28 mm in length, considerably larger than those of the bluebird.

Wood Mouse, White-footed Mouse, Deer Mouse
(Peromyscus leucopus)

This beautiful big-eyed native mouse, with a tawny to nearly orange coat and pure white underparts, is a frequent resident in the bluebird box. An excellent climber, the mouse has no trouble with a steel fence post or even the vertical wires of mesh fencing. Wood mice are most at home in the woods or anyplace with good cover—logs, hollow trees, rocks, crevices, trash, and brush. However, we have had them take up residence in boxes along clean pasture fences a hundred yards or more from any cover other than the box.

Although mice will sometimes raise young in the boxes in summer, their heavy usage is during the coldest months. The mice will fill a box with soft fluffy material such as milkweed down, fur, shredded plant fibers, cotton, wool, and shredded paper. This provides excellent insulation for the completely closed chamber in the middle, where several adult mice may sleep through the cold winter days. Being nocturnal creatures, the mice are usually at home when the bluebirder comes to check on his boxes in late winter in preparation for the arrival of his featured guests. Wood mice are gentle creatures, easily handled, and reluctant to bite. They make excellent pets, more interesting than hamsters and gerbils, and will readily take to the exercise wheel in your hamster cage. Unfortunately, the recent discovery of the hantavirus carried by mice has made it potentially dangerous to handle these animals. When cleaning out a mouse nest avoid touching the material or breathing any dust that may arise.

Mouse populations fluctuate dramatically. Some years you will have none, while in other years they will become a problem on your

A wood mouse has taken over this box.

bluebird trail. During the winter of 1989-90 mice built nests in nearly every box along the highways in Kentucky, several boxes containing as many as seven adults.

During your spring housecleaning, you should remove the mouse nests and expel the mice. Bluebirds seem to be dominant over mice and will build atop a mouse nest, sometimes even laying their eggs on the soft mouse nest without adding any nesting material. Bluebirds are much more likely, however, to use the box if the mouse nest is removed. Also, the mess of urine and feces beneath the nest is likely to rot the floor if not cleaned out. Use a large screwdriver or similar tool to remove a mouse nest.

Mice usually abandon a box after being routed in early spring. Some individuals, however, are persistent. When this happens it may be necessary to move the box from the post, wire it to the fence, and treat the fence with Tangle Trap, a sticky substance designed as a barrier for crawling insects. When using Tangle Trap, be careful to avoid getting it where the bluebirds might get into it. Bluebirds will perch on the

*The acrobatic
flying squirrel*

top strand of the fence or on the box. Unfortunately, Tangle Trap may not always deter mice. Although we have yet to have mice go through it during the bluebird breeding season, they readily enter the boxes in winter, actually wearing away the Tangle Trap with their traffic. Tangle Trap may be obtained from a farm supply dealer or from the Tanglefoot Corporation; see the Appendix for more information.

An alternative is to trap persistent mice. Wood mice are easily captured in either live traps or snap traps baited with rolled oats.

Southern Flying Squirrel *(Glaucomys volans)*

One of the most attractive of our native mammals, the big-eyed, velvety-furred flying squirrel is an occasional visitor at the bluebird box. Strictly nocturnal, he will be at home asleep when you visit the box and, after dashing out into the sunshine, he is likely to decide he picked the wrong site for his nap.

Flying squirrels are arboreal and not found far from woodlands or scattered trees. They are most likely to be found in boxes nailed to trees, one of the least favorable sites for your bluebirds. Boxes at the edge of a young woodlot, where trees are too young to provide natural cavities, are also good candidates for flying squirrel activity. Flying squirrels sometimes destroy the eggs and young of bluebirds and take over a nest box.

The southern flying squirrel can enter any bluebird box without enlarging the opening, whereas the larger northern flying squirrel (*Glaucomys sabrinus*), found in the northernmost states and Canada, usually needs to do some chewing.

Bats

Apparently several kinds of bats during their nightly wanderings visit and explore bluebird boxes. Evidence of their activity is seen as slim droppings consisting entirely of the chitinous exoskeletons of insects. On the reclaimed surface mines of eastern Kentucky, single northern bats (*Myotis septentrionalis*) would sometimes occupy our boxes during the day (Moriarty and Davis 1984). We have also had the common little brown bat (*Myotis lucifugus*) take up residence in one of our bluebird boxes (Davis and Dourson 1991), and we have seen signs of big brown bats (*Eptesicus fuscus*) in several.

Our several bat species found in most of the United States are entirely insectivorous. Most bats are declining in numbers and several are endangered species. Thus bat use of our boxes should be encouraged. Several special housing structures can be built for bats. See Appendix for additional information on bat conservation.

Gray Tree Frog *(Hyla versicolor)*

On the surface mines, where breeding ponds were available but where there were no trees or shrubs in some areas, we have had tree frogs take up residence in our bluebird boxes. A tree frog is harmless and probably would not deter a bluebird that wanted to use the box. However, you may choose to remove a frog and take it to a woods or pond.

Ants

Several species of ants invade bluebird houses; we have had five species living in our boxes in Kentucky. Ants are the most serious problem we encounter on some of our bluebird trails.

In the Deep South, the fire ant *(Solenopsis germinata)* is a major problem. This alien species, imported from South America and established at Mobile, Alabama, has spread along the coastal states from the Carolinas to Texas. Their northward spread is limited by their inability to tolerate cold weather. Fire ants present a special problem; not only are they a threat to bluebirds but they inflict a painful sting on people. A pustule develops at the site of the sting and remains painful for several days.

Although fire ants do not live in bluebird boxes, their persistent explorations lead to their discovery of the nest and young. According to Dew et al. (1986), the fire ants leave only skeletons and feathers and an abandoned box. Fire ants live in large conspicuous earthen mounds. If one of these is near your bluebird box, you should take care to protect it from the ants.

We do not have fire ants in Kentucky, but we have serious problems with a nasty little biting ant *(Crematogaster clara)*. One of our most abundant species, these ants take up residence in any enclosed area that provides protection from the rain. A favored nest site is in the bags of leaves I pile up next to my garden. They have nested in the wall of my house, entering via a tiny opening beside the outdoor faucet. I have seen them living in the dry hollow stalks from last year's poke *(Phytolacca americana)* and other rank weeds. The species was originally described from colonies living in oak galls in Texas. They reside in cans, bottles, and other trash along the highways.

As the ant colony grows, it may outgrow its living space, such as that provided by a smashed beer can, and explorers will begin looking for a new home. A bluebird box on the fence seems ideal and the colony moves in. It matters not whether the box is empty or contains a bird nest. In an empty box the white eggs, larvae, and pupae simply lie on the floor where they may cover the entire surface. The workers proceed to make carton, a paperlike substance they produce by chew-

Carton, produced by ants, fills the entrance to this box.

ing up the wood of the box. We have seen the slot entrances of boxes entirely closed off by carton.

If a bird nest is in the box, the ants make little or no carton. Most ant eggs will be located on the floor under the nest, although they are often also distributed up into the grass of the bluebird nest. Ants are usually obvious, swarming out as soon as the box is opened.

Crematogaster clara is a distinctive species. It is dark, almost black. The abdomen is a deep chocolate brown, nearly black, and the rest of the body is slightly paler and somewhat reddish. The workers are about 3.5 mm long. When agitated, this species raises the abdomen, pointing it into the air.

If young bluebirds are in the nest when ants invade, they often coexist and the young fledge; they are not abandoned. If ants invade during nest construction or when eggs are present, however, bluebirds nearly always abandon. Nests in these stages should always be checked for ants because sometimes they are not obvious. Run a screwdriver beneath the nest along both edges of the floor; this will stir up ants if they are present.

Ant problems may begin in May and will increase throughout

Ants

the summer as more colonies outgrow their quarters and move into the boxes. If heavy spring rains occur, ants may invade sooner and take over more boxes as they are driven from shelters on the ground. We have had stretches of highway in Kentucky where nearly every box was taken by ants and all bluebird nests abandoned.

Fortunately, it is usually easy to construct a barrier to prevent access to the box by ants. For this one should purchase a can of Tangle Trap. One application of this material has remained effective where we have had it in place for over three years. Various greases and oils have been recommended, but they do not last and must be reapplied several times during a season. Krueger (1989) makes an ant barrier by mixing a quart of turpentine with five pounds of chassis grease. For a smaller quantity, try seven ounces of turpentine to one pound of chassis grease. Krueger found that this mixture would last throughout the bluebird breeding season.

Tangle Trap must be placed carefully to avoid the possibility that bluebirds might come into contact with it. If you are putting boxes on a mesh fence topped with a strand of barbed wire, fasten the box to the top strand of the mesh. Avoid the barbed wire because it tends to rust and break, and the strain of supporting the box may hasten that process. Also, bluebirds perch on the top of fences, and you should avoid putting Tangle Trap on the top strand. If the barbed strand is low enough to touch your box, thus allowing access to ants, loosen a fastener on a post and raise it a notch.

Although bluebirds perch on the top of a fence, chickadees, house wrens, and house sparrows will use the lower strands. There have been reports of chickadees being caught in the Tangle Trap. To avoid this problem, keep it close to the box, too close to allow perching space to encroach. It does not take much of a barrier to deter ants; however the material slowly oxidizes, so I try to get a generous amount in place.

To deter ants in a box to be nailed to a post, cut one-inch pieces of tubing such as plastic pipe or copper water pipe, one piece for each nail to be used. Put the tubing between the box and the post with the nails running through the tubes. This separates the box from the post. Put Tangle Trap on the tubing, the only points of access for ants.

Although Tangle Trap or Krueger's grease mixture will deter the ants, it occasionally is circumvented. A tall weed or grass head touching the box will provide access, and the ants will quickly discover it. Weeds should be pulled away or cut back if they are about to touch the box. Of course, in erecting boxes you should always use areas where no vines are growing. Not only do they provide access to ants, but bluebirds do not like leafy vegetation around the box.

Ants live in the boxes only during the summer. In the autumn the entire colony moves out. If you have boxes that you check only once a year and clean out in late winter, you may be unaware of an ant problem because they sometimes leave no sign of their previous occupation, especially if there was a bird nest in the box.

Since ants must have shelter for the winter, you can avoid an ant problem by carefully selecting sites for your bluebird boxes. Weeds, logs, trash, and rocks provide winter cover for ants. Areas that are mowed or pastured with clean fence rows are least likely to shelter the kinds of ants that inhabit bluebird boxes.

Wasps *(Polistes* sp.)

Paper wasps that build their paper nests in various sheltered places, such as beneath the awnings over your windows, like the protected nest sites provided by bluebird boxes. In Kentucky in recent years our common paper wasp has been supplemented by a European import, which is slightly larger and not as dark and also likes bluebird boxes.

Fortunately, wasps are seldom a problem on the bluebird trail. The birds seem in control; wasps do not establish nests in boxes occupied by bluebirds. Wasps tend to nest in the boxes late in the season and take up residence in boxes that are empty. Although these wasps can sting, they are not aggressive, and one can simply knock the nest down with a screwdriver or a stick. The nest is usually built beneath the roof but occasionally on one of the sides. If the nest is removed, the wasps desert the site. If the nest is not destroyed, a colony of wasps develops. They can become aggressive and probably can keep out the bluebirds. I have seen wasp nests that entirely covered the roofs of boxes.

Bumblebees *(Bombus* sp.)

Bumblebees are aggressive. They will attack when you open the box and may quickly drive you away. Your only options are to abandon the site for the season or return at night to destroy the bees. You can spray the bees with a household bug bomb and remove the nest.

Fortunately, bumblebees seldom inhabit bluebird boxes. When they do, they choose the soft nest of a mouse, chickadee, or titmouse and make their nest chamber inside the fluffy material. Their buzzing is usually audible before the bees attack.

Blowflies (Apaulina sialia)

In several species of parasitic flies, the larvae inhabit the nests of birds and feed on the blood of the nestlings. Your first encounter with the blowfly that commonly attacks bluebirds is likely to be when you approach a box a week or so after the young have fledged. Although you don't get a very good look at the flies, they behave like ordinary carrion flies, and you are likely to expect to find a maggot-riddled dead bird in the box. Instead, you find only an empty nest where the young bluebirds have fledged.

If you lift out the old nest, you will find embedded in the bottom of it the brown pupa cases of the blowflies. They are oval-shaped and a little more than a quarter of an inch long. The adult female blowfly lays eggs in the nesting material in the bluebird box. These develop into maggots that live in the nest. They attack the young bluebirds at night, feeding on blood, retreating into the nesting material by day. When the larvae are mature, they are plump gray maggots about half an inch long.

Blowflies are rarely a problem. We often encounter a dozen or more pupa cases in boxes where healthy young bluebirds have fledged. Apparently, occasionally blowfly larvae are numerous enough to cause weakening or even death of the young. Fifty or more larvae are said to be cause for concern. If young birds appear weak or sickly you might want to check for parasitic maggots. Lift out the nest. Maggots will begin to drop out. You can shake out most of them or spray the nest with a pyrethrin spray for canaries available at your pet store. The best and easiest solution, however, is to make a crude nest with dry grass and replace the young in it. This is the best solution to any nest problem when there are young: ants, lice, mites, maggots, wet nest. Both the youngsters and the parents will readily accept your handiwork. Some trail monitors always make new nests for young bluebirds to eliminate the blowflies.

Pinkowski (1977b) found his bluebird nests in Michigan heavily parasitized with an average of ninety-one fly pupae per infested box. He reported that unless the numbers were 130 or more that the parasites did not affect survival of the young bluebirds. Wittmann and Beason (1992) and Roby et al. (1992) also studied parasitic blowflies and found they had little or no detrimental effect on the young bluebirds.

Blowfly populations are controlled in part by a tiny parasitic wasp *(Nasonia vitripennis)*. These wasps lay eggs on the pupae of the blowflies. The larvae that hatch feed on the developing blowfly, and tiny adult wasps emerge from the pupa case. Unfortunately, you cannot tell by inspecting the pupa whether it has been parasitized or not.

Darling and Thomson-Delaney (1993) studied the ecology of the blowflies and their tiny wasp parasites. The flies overwinter as adults, not in the boxes, whereas the wasps overwinter as larvae in the fly pupae. Thus the standard practice of cleaning out old bluebird nests in the fall or early spring probably increases the blowfly population. We have found that bluebirds have a strong preference for boxes containing old nests (Davis et al. 1994). Thus, in regions where blowflies are a problem, it may be best to leave old nests in the boxes.

Mites

All kinds of birds have parasitic mites. In many birds the nest is crawling with thousands of mites just after the young have fledged. For some strange reason this apparently does not happen with bluebirds; few mites are ever found in the old nest. Bluebirds are about the only birds that return to the same site to raise a second brood in the same season; the absence of mite problems is likely important for this behavior.

If you encounter mites in a box after the young have fledged, remove the old nest and carry it away. Brush out mites from the box or spray lightly with a spray from your pet store intended for use on birds. If you want to avoid putting insect spray into a nesting chamber, an alternative is to replace the box with a new one, take the mite infested one home, and give it a bath with detergent.

Checking the boxes on a bluebird trail is always an interesting experience. You never know what you will find when you open a box. You will encounter a diversity of fascinating creatures and get a real introduction to our natural world.

8

Foiling House Sparrows

HOUSE SPARROWS *(Passer domesticus)* are generally considered the most serious problem for people trying to establish bluebirds. Sparrows can enter any cavity accessible to bluebirds and these ubiquitous pests may take over all of your boxes if you don't plan properly. Sparrows will evict bluebirds, sometimes killing an adult in a box (Gowaty 1984). They will fill the box with trash, building their nest on the eggs or small young of the bluebirds. Larger young are often pecked to death by the sparrows before the nest is built over them. Kridler (1991) reported that one year sparrows killed twenty-six adult bluebirds and destroyed over 150 eggs and young on his trail in Texas.

A male (left) and female house sparrow

Although sparrows do not eat the eggs and young, they may be considered predators as well as competitors because they will peck and destroy eggs, young, and adult bluebirds. I used to think that they attacked bluebirds only if they wanted the nest site. However, I once watched an adult male house sparrow enter a box, where it pecked a hole in a bluebird egg and left. The sparrow showed no further interest in that experimental box, which was designed to be unsuitable for sparrows. Fortunately, most house sparrows do not bother nesting bluebirds; it is apparently only an occasional individual that causes problems.

The one sure way to avoid sparrow problems is to place your boxes where there are no house sparrows. If you are making a trail of boxes across the countryside this is usually easy to do, for house sparrows are strongly associated with people and buildings, and most good bluebird habitat is found where there are no sparrows. Sites half a mile or more from buildings are usually free of sparrows.

Most people interested in attracting bluebirds, however, would like to get them to nest near their home. If you want to entice bluebirds to your yard, you will very likely have to deal with the house sparrow problem. There are two general methods that are successful. You can trap and destroy the sparrows, or you can design and place boxes in such a way that they are of little interest to sparrows. If you live in the city, trapping appears to be the only hope. People in Minnesota, Wisconsin, and Ohio have succeeded in enticing bluebirds back into some parts of cities with diligent programs of trapping and destroying house sparrows. We have been unable to get them into suitable habitat in Lexington, Kentucky, however, despite our efforts with boxes designed and placed so as to discourage house sparrows.

House sparrows that have taken over a bluebird house are rather easily trapped in the box. If your box has a standard circular entrance, you can buy or build a Huber trap or Gilbertson trap or make the very simple Stutchbury trap. See chapter 11. A slot entrance box is not amenable to these traps, however. A simple method that works in any box is a sticky mouse trap available at any hardware, farm supply, or general department store. You must watch carefully to avoid catching a desirable species and remove the trap as soon as the house

A house sparrow nest and young

sparrow is caught. House sparrows are not protected by law. You can easily kill a sparrow by compressing the lungs with a finger on each side of the breast just beneath the wings.

For those who do not want to trap and kill house sparrows, there are alternatives. Although the problem cannot be eliminated, it can be considerably alleviated by placement of boxes and box design. Place your boxes low, about four or five feet above ground, on posts in the open. House sparrows prefer higher nest sites and bluebirds are just as likely to use a low site as a higher one. Bluebirds will readily use a box three or even two feet above ground, and the lower the box the less likely it will be taken by sparrows. Lower boxes, however, are more likely to be found by predators and are more difficult to protect from predators. If raccoons and house cats are not a problem but house sparrows are, you might consider placing your boxes about three feet above the ground.

There are various kinds of nesting structures that bluebirds will use and house sparrows do not like. Paper milk cartons and various plastic containers are sometimes used by bluebirds and rarely, if ever, by house sparrows. Paper cartons last only a season, plastic produces heat problems unless well ventilated, and bluebirds prefer wooden boxes (Davis 1989a). We have had success with paper cartons in some areas. You may want to try them. See chapter 11.

Research at the University of Kentucky has shown that bluebirds prefer a box with a slot entrance over one with a circular entrance (McComb et al. 1987) and that house sparrows have a preference for the circular entrance (Davis 1989b). House sparrows also like a deep and roomy box that they can fill with trash to make their bulky nest. Based on this information, we have built three types of boxes that are useful in alleviating the house sparrow problem.

A slot entrance box with a floor of 4 x 4 or 3½ x 4 inches and a depth of three to four inches from the bottom of the entrance to the floor is seldom used by sparrows. The more shallow the box is, the

A good spot for bluebirds

less likely that sparrows will take it. Apparently Baxter (1982) was the first to suggest that a shallow box may be suitable for bluebirds but not for house sparrows. Bluebirds are less likely to use a box as the depth gets less than four inches, however. The best system is to build a standard Kentucky bluebird box, as described in chapter 11, which is five inches deep. If sparrows are a problem, put in a piece of a two-by-four to make the depth only 3½ inches. A box with these dimensions is rarely used by house sparrows (Davis 1991).

Some people have expressed concern that the young may fledge too soon from a shallow box. This does not seem likely, however. Young bluebirds do not ordinarily leave the box on their own; they have to be coaxed out by the parents when the parents have decided it is time for them to leave.

Zeleny (1976) suggested that a box should be at least six inches deep to avoid problems from starlings. With a shallow box a starling could reach in and destroy eggs, young, or an incubating bluebird. It is most unusual for this to actually happen; there is one report of it in the literature (Lippy 1993). Even when boxes are made accessible to starlings, the starlings seldom bother nesting bluebirds (Davis et al. 1986; Davis and McComb 1989). Even if you have occasional problems with starlings, the fact that house sparrows do not seem to be interested in a shallow box may be more important.

You can make another sparrow-inhibiting box with the Kentucky bluebird box design by simply dropping the front down an extra inch, making a large entrance 2 x 3½ inches and with a depth of four inches. This box, however, is accessible to starlings; although they show little interest in such a box there is a possibility that they may destroy the eggs or young of bluebirds.

Steve Gilbertson (1991; 1993) developed a sparrow-inhibiting box using thin polyvinyl chloride (PVC) four-inch sewer pipe. We ran tests on this box built with a slot entrance and a depth of 4½ inches and found that sparrows rarely used it. More important, we found that bluebirds liked it as well as a standard box, a feature not found with our other sparrow-inhibiting boxes (Davis and Mack 1994). We recommend the Gilbertson box as the best sparrow-inhibiting box that has yet been designed.

Most bluebird trails are along highways.

With all sparrow-inhibiting boxes, it is common for a male house sparrow to adopt the box, especially early in the season. He will bring in a few sprigs of grass and will spend most of the day sitting on or beside the box and chirping. The usual pattern is for him to decide that the site is too marginal and abandon it in two or three days. In the rare case that he attracts a mate and they seriously start to build a nest, you can put in a piece of wood to make the box more shallow until they abandon the site.

Vincent Bauldry in Wisconsin designed a box meant to discourage sparrows. An opening three inches in diameter is made in the roof, then covered with hardware cloth to let in extra light. We have found, however, that sparrows do use the box and that the opening admits water, sometimes soaking the nest. We tried a Plexiglas skylight but found that bluebirds did not like it. It had no effect on the sparrows.

Gowaty (1981) has shown that if an empty box is available house sparrows will usually take it rather than evicting bluebirds and that the farther along the bluebirds are in their breeding the less likely they are to be evicted by sparrows. Because sparrows seldom bother bluebirds unless they are interested in taking the box for their own nest, the best insurance against house sparrow problems is a properly designed box placed low on a post or wired to a fence, with another box available nearby. It would be unusual for sparrows to take both boxes.

So, if you don't want to kill house sparrows, the most effective way to deal with the problem is to always to have more than one box. Although eviction of nesting bluebirds by house sparrows is not very common, it can be extremely distressing to a person who has bluebirds nesting in a single box in the yard. Even if the sparrows are trapped and destroyed, the bluebirds will not return until after the sparrows and their nest are removed; if there is another box in the vicinity, however, the bluebirds will have already moved into it by the time you discover the sparrow problem. The experience with the sparrows will be only a minor setback for the bluebirds if a second box is available.

9
Predators

PEOPLE ARE LIKELY to be upset and angry when checking up on a family of bluebirds whose progress they have followed for weeks only to discover the nest destroyed and feathers and parts of young and adult bluebirds scattered beneath the box. Nearly everyone who has had much experience with bluebird boxes has occasionally encountered this sad situation. People have devised a wide variety of tactics to try to decrease or eliminate the predation problem. Nearly all the literature on the numerous ideas for deterring predators consists of simple anecdotes; somebody tries something and says it works. There is a need for controlled experiments to test these various ideas to see which ones really work.

The natural reaction of most people is probably to want to destroy the predator or do whatever is necessary to prevent a recurrence. Of course, if you are dealing with a bluebird family nesting in a box in your yard where you like to watch them from your house, it is understandable that you may want to go to elaborate or even costly means to protect them from predation. If you have a trail of a number of boxes across the countryside, however, you should try to develop a different attitude.

Predation is a fact of nature. The most serious predators at the bluebird nest are black rat snakes *(Elaphe obsoleta)* and raccoons *(Procyon lotor)*. Both are native animals, part of the normal balance of nature, necessary for the normal control of the populations of prey species. Bluebirds are so productive that, even if predators raid half the nests on your trail, the bluebird population will still have increased considerably. And there are some simple things that you can do to reduce the rate of predation at your boxes.

Snakes

Throughout most of the range of the eastern bluebird, snakes are major predators at the nest. The problem becomes less severe northward and drops out entirely in the northernmost portion of the range, where predatory snakes do not occur.

Snakes leave no sign of having raided the box, and if one is not familiar with them their activity can seem mysterious. For example, if you are checking your boxes weekly you may find five eggs, one egg, and five eggs on successive visits, or perhaps five eggs, an empty nest, three eggs, then five eggs. Another sign is to find five eggs three or even four weeks in a row and think them either infertile or abandoned only to find young birds on the fifth week. In each of the above cases a snake has taken one clutch and the bluebird simply proceeded to lay a second. It is routine for a bluebird to lay a new clutch in the same nest after a snake has taken the eggs. Fortunately, snakes do not seem to have very good memories and the new clutch is frequently successful. We once found a snake coiled in a box where it had eaten a clutch of five eggs, and the following week the bluebird was incubating four eggs from which she successfully fledged young.

Snakes frequently take young that are near fledging. In our studies of snake predation (Davis and McComb 1988), we found that exploring snakes occasionally visited empty boxes. We suspect that they somehow know that there are young birds in a box because they so frequently took large young. The bluebird trail monitor probably often records that young have fledged when actually they have been eaten by a snake.

Another indication of snake predation is a new nest too soon in a box. When you record young fledged at a box and find a new nest the very next week, the young were probably taken by a snake. When young fledge successfully, the parents usually start their nest for the next brood from two to six weeks later.

Laskey (1946) found that snakes took the eggs and young from about half the nestings she had in her boxes in the city parks in Nashville. She was able to detect snake predation by visiting her boxes daily and keeping careful records. In Kentucky, we find that snakes are often the most common predators and second only to ants as the major problem at the boxes. In our studies we could recognize snake visits by the fact that snakes went through the Tangle Trap we put on the posts and smeared it on the boxes. We recorded heavy predations by snakes at our boxes on the mines in eastern Kentucky.

The black rat snake or pilot black snake *(Elaphe obsoleta)* is a very common predatory snake throughout its range of most parts of the eastern United States. It is an arboreal snake that spends much of its time in trees seeking the eggs and young of birds, which form a major part of its diet. A prolonged cacophony of forest birds, objecting as all birds do when a predator threatens their young, can usually be traced to a black rat snake raiding a nest in a tree.

In the daytime, black rat snakes are often found foraging on the ground in the cool forest, though in the hottest weather they usually retreat into tree cavities. Although such retreats are usually in the forest, these snakes will occasionally, at least temporarily, dwell in old hollow trees out in the field.

In the cool of the night, black rat snakes wander out away from the forest in search of prey. In our studies on the reclaimed surface mines in eastern Kentucky, where the deciduous forest abruptly meets extensive grasslands, we found that boxes placed near the forest edge were most often raided but that boxes much farther than one hundred yards from the woods appeared to be safe.

Black rat snakes are superb climbers, and various efforts by numerous people to devise means of preventing them from reaching bluebird boxes have generally been unsuccessful. They can climb any pole of any size, no matter how smooth, even if coated with grease. Tangle Trap, which deters other predators, seems to have no effect. At five to six feet long, a mature black snake has no trouble breaching an inverted cone made of a circle of sheet metal a yard in diameter.

Efforts to deter snake predation include placing a strip of carpet tacks with the points outward around the post supporting the box (Dupree and Wright 1990). Tack strips are inexpensive and are available at carpet stores. This idea looks promising but needs further testing.

Paterson (1988) claimed that a five-foot length of aluminum downspout or PVC pipe four inches in diameter placed over the mounting pipe deters snakes. Harry Krueger found that a section of PVC pipe placed over the mounting pipe does not deter snakes, and he has a photograph to prove it. Richard Peterson claims that a twenty-four-inch piece of 1½- or two-inch PVC pipe placed over the mounting posts just beneath the box stops all climbing predators.

Jack Finch ran extensive tests. He placed dozens of large rat snakes in a pen; to escape they would have had to climb a pole covered with a five-foot length of PVC pipe four inches in diameter. With loose fine sand on the ground at the base of the pole (so that the snakes could not brace themselves with their tails), none escaped. Without the sand, a couple of them succeeded in climbing out.

When placing your boxes, keep snake predation in mind and try to locate them as far from the woods as feasible. There may be an inverse relationship between the distance from woods and the frequency of predation by black rat snakes. Keeping boxes away from the woods also lowers the probability that house wrens or flying squirrels will evict your bluebirds.

The black racer *(Coluber constrictor)*, common throughout the eastern and midwestern states, also raids bluebird boxes. Its habits and habitat are quite different from those of the black rat snake. Racers are diurnal and thus much more likely to be seen by people checking bluebird boxes. They prefer the open country to the dense forest. Favored habitat includes unmowed grass and weeds with scattered shrubs and open woods with an unmowed understory of grass and shrubs. Such areas are also good bluebird habitat. Racers do not like heavily grazed or mowed lands that do not provide adequate cover.

In the prairie states, the bull snake *(Pituophis melanoleucus)* is a predator of bluebirds. Several other climbing snakes, such as the coachwhip *(Masticophis flagellum)* and the milk snake *(Lampropeltis doliata)*, probably occasionally visit the bluebird box for an easy meal. Even the garter snake *(Thamnophis sirtalis)* has been known to climb into a box and eat bluebird eggs (Caldwell 1991).

On rare occasions you may encounter a snake in a bluebird box. Black rat snakes, which feed mostly at night, nearly always leave the box. Occasionally, however, one will curl up in the box to digest its meal and you will discover it when you make your rounds. Sometimes you will see the snake's head protruding from the entrance. The snake may be looking around as if it has just awakened after a gluttonous meal and is wondering what it is doing out in an open field in the daytime. On other occasions you may open a box and find a drowsy rat snake coiled tightly therein. For people who do not like such surprises, one of the advantages of a 4 x 4-inch floor dimension and a shallow box is that a big rat snake is less likely to stay as long as it might if the box were larger.

On the occasions that I have found a snake at one of my boxes I have left it alone. Although snakes are not protected by law, they are a part of the natural balance of nature and should not be killed. As a compromise between killing one and leaving it alone you might consider removing it and releasing it in the woods several miles away.

Rat snakes may threaten at first but are quite gentle. They tame quickly and actually seem to enjoy being handled. Racers, on the other hand, have nasty tempers, will threaten when cornered, are not at all reluctant to bite, and do not become tame with handling.

The late Harry Krueger (1991a) developed a snake trap to deploy at his bluebird boxes. His design consists of garden netting gathered at the pole and skirted at the bottom edge with a circular piece of wire to hold it out away from the pole. Snakes climb up under the netting and get entangled. Krueger caught the snakes, sometimes as many as three at one site, carried them away, and released them. The system is very effective; however, you must monitor it closely because bluebirds will not enter a box when there is a snake in the netting. See chapter 11 for instructions on building Krueger's snake guard.

Raccoons *(Procyon lotor)*

The raccoon, a nocturnal predatory carnivore, is very common and widely distributed across much of North America. They are strong and intelligent, excellent climbers, and usually spend their days in hollow trees. Raccoons have dexterous forepaws and are much more adept at raiding bluebird boxes than are house cats.

The feeding of raccoons is heavily associated with water (Kennedy et al. 1991). Raccoon tracks can be seen in the mud beside almost any stream or pond within their range. They feed mostly on crayfish, frogs, tadpoles, and minnows, but they venture into the uplands to feed on birds' eggs and young and any other edibles they can find. Raccoons nearly always begin an evening's forage at the water's edge and have their feet well covered with mud by the time they visit the bluebird house. A casual inspection at the site of the crime will usually tell you if a raccoon is your culprit; they nearly always leave a conspicuous amount of mud on the box and on the post or fence upon which the box is mounted. You may also find bits of fur caught in splinters on the post or the box or on barbed wire, and claw marks on the sides and roof of the box. If the box has a circular entrance, the raccoon will pull part of the nest out through the hole, leaving a conspicuous wad of dry grass protruding. With a slot entrance box, a raccoon will sometimes remove the entire nest; in other instances a raccoon will scoop out the eggs or young while leaving the surface of the nest only mildly disturbed. Often a raccoon will kill and eat the incubating female bluebird and leave the eggs in the box, sometimes broken and sometimes not. The feathers of the female bluebird will be on the ground beneath the box.

Problems with raccoons are quite variable. The closer a box is to the water, the more likely it will be raided by raccoons. Bluebird trails in many upland areas have no problems with raccoons. A trail may go for several years with no problem and then be discovered by a raccoon. A raccoon may work along a trail and raid several boxes in a row, ranging as far as half a mile. Unlike snakes, raccoons seem to have a good memory and will raid the same box repeatedly. If you clean out a box after a raccoon has raided it the bluebirds will usually nest again; however, unless something is done to deter the predator, it is likely to return.

At some parks and campgrounds raccoons become so abundant that bluebird boxes would have no success unless protected from predators. A person must look at each situation when planning a bluebird trail to decide whether to go to the extra trouble and expense of trying to deter predators. It may be that there will be some sites where you will want to install predator guards and others where they are not needed. Or you may simply want to wait and see if you are going to have significant predator problems. In many areas predation is so light that it can be ignored. Boxes on fences are more likely to be raided by raccoons than boxes on power poles.

Devices for deterring raccoons fall into two categories: things to prevent the raccoon from getting at the birds in the box, and those that prevent it from getting to the box. In general, the former tend to be simple and cheap and the latter require more effort and expense. Unfortunately, at least an occasional raccoon can foil any of the exclusion devices, and bluebirds dislike most of them. If a good exclusion device is ever developed, it will make fences much more attractive sites for your bluebird boxes.

Keeping raccoons from getting to your boxes is more desirable than allowing them to reach the boxes and then trying to prevent them from reaching the birds inside. Curtis (1991) writes that he does not want raccoons on his boxes because he suspects that a raccoon climbing on a box might cause the bluebirds to desert their nest. This seems a reasonable possibility.

Several methods of keeping raccoons from reaching the boxes are apparently successful. A disadvantage is that all require the expense of setting a post or pipe; at many good sites this cannot be done because it would interfere with mowing. The most popular method is to mount the box on a steel pipe and treat the pipe with a mixture made of five pounds of chassis grease and a quart of turpentine. This substance has the added advantage of keeping out ants. To be effective against raccoons, grease must be applied liberally over the length of the pole. Raccoons and cattle will lick off any grease that they can reach.

There are ways of avoiding undue expense for mounting pipe. Dick Tuttle takes a pipe cutter to a place where they are demolishing an old building and salvages water pipe and gas pipe in pieces about seven feet long. E.J. Schaefer in Minnesota gets 1½-inch pipe from well drillers, who are often glad to get rid of their used pipe. Harry Krueger bought three-quarter-inch water pipe in ten-foot lengths threaded on both ends. He cut each length into one six-foot and one four-foot section, then used a coupling to join the two.

Avoiding mowing machines is a problem. Probably most of us

who have a trail with boxes mounted on pipes have had an occasional incidence of scrambled eggs. Harry Krueger had his boxes along
the Texas highways in the mowed rights-of-way. He carried his lawn
mower and cut a wide circle around each box. He also elicited the
cooperation of the mowing contractor. An alternative is to mount your
pipes next to structures that the mowers must avoid, such as culverts,
tombstones, and support cables of power poles.

People have come up with many ideas for protecting bluebird
houses from raccoon predation. The most commonly used method is
to add a piece of wood to the front door, doubling the thickness of the
door at the entrance. A piece of wood is drilled with a 1½-inch hole
that fits over the entrance of the same diameter and this piece is glued
or fastened with screws to the front of the box. The idea is that with
the added thickness the raccoon will not be able to reach through the
hole and down into the nest. Unfortunately, however, this popular
system does not work. Berner et al. (1990) found that a raccoon had
no difficulty removing food from the bottom of a box that had a three-
quarter-inch predator guard over the entrance of a box made of three-
quarter-inch lumber (thus making the thickness at the entrance 1½
inches). One might think that the problem could be solved by making
the entrance passage even longer, but bluebirds do not like to enter a
tunnel and will usually reject an entrance of wood more than 1½ inches
thick. Sedlacek (1987) found that he could add another layer of predator guard, making it nearly three inches thick, if he added it after
there were eggs or young in the nest, and the bluebirds would not
abandon. Don Wilkins gives the raccoons an extra problem by his
method of drilling an entrance hole. Instead of drilling perpendicu-
larly, he slants the entrance hole upward. Frank Zuern (1994) has designed a horizontal box in which the bluebirds nest at the far end beyond the reach of a raccoon. See chapter 11 for plans for Zuern's box.

A plastic attachment known as the "Bird Guardian," distributed
by Audubon Entities, is an entrance extension that sticks out three
inches in front of the box. Berner et al. (1990) found that this device
deterred raccoons. Berner (1990) learned, however, that bluebirds will
not use a box equipped with such a device. The Bird Guardian has
been modified and improved, but Berner (1991) still does not recom-

mend it; bluebirds don't like it. However, Daughrity (1991) reported that the new Bird Guardian was accepted by bluebirds on all her boxes.

Another idea is to make a deep box with a wooden predator guard over the entrance hole in hopes that a raccoon will have trouble reaching the nest. Unfortunately, with a deep box, bluebirds often build a deeper nest so that their eggs and young are still near the entrance. Read (1989) solved this problem by lowering the nest. With young in the nest or eggs near hatching, he removed the bottom part of the nest and lowered the remainder. Read thought that this action in combination with his wooden predator guard at the entrance deterred raccoons. His boxes were 8½ to nine inches deep from entrance to floor.

Unfortunately, the combination of a wooden predator guard and a deep box is not attractive to bluebirds. Many people in the bluebird recovery program in Wisconsin use such boxes. This may be the reason that the Wisconsin program has such a low rate of occupancy. The wooden predator guard probably should not be used.

Various other attachments to the entrance have been developed (e.g., Noel 1991; Hutchings 1991) as predator guards. Some of these apparently deter most raccoons; however, bluebirds do not like them and they should not be placed until the clutch is complete or young are in the box and the adults are reluctant to abandon.

One would think that mounting a box on a smooth pipe such as PVC would prevent a raccoon from climbing to the box. Berner et al. (1990) and Curtis (1991) found that their raccoons had no trouble getting to boxes mounted on steel pipe or PVC pipe ⅞ inch and 1½ inches in diameter. Bruss (1990) found that raccoons apparently climbed her four-inch PVC pipes. Berner et al. (1990) found that boxes with the roofs extending seven inches forward over the entrance and mounted on pipes gave their raccoon difficulty, although he eventually was able to solve it.

Mounting boxes on pipe and smearing the pipe with grease or Tangle Trap will deter most raccoons. We had no problem with raccoons when we mounted boxes on steel T-posts and smeared the posts just beneath the boxes with Tangle Trap. We sometimes found raccoon fur in the Tangle Trap, but the bluebird nests were unharmed. Unfortunately, however, we once found the feathers of a male bluebird and a flicker in the Tangle Trap and suspect that these birds did not survive the experience. Others have reported that grease on the pole did not deter their raccoons. We have occasionally had raccoons climb smooth electric conduit, going through the grease to raid bluebird nests.

Richard Peterson has been experimenting with a simple and inexpensive device to try to deter raccoons and house cats. He drills two holes into the front of the box on the inside an inch apart and just beneath the entrance. Into these he inserts pieces of wooden dowels so that they project 1½ inches into the box. This apparently does not bother the bluebirds. The idea is that the predator would have trouble reaching down past the dowels to the nest. Unfortunately, at least some raccoons have mastered the puzzle, and Peterson is modifying his design. Perhaps three or four dowels placed a half inch apart might work.

Schweikert (1988) has come up with an unusual idea that just might work to deter raccoons. She ties five or six shoots of multiflora rose to the fence posts on which she has boxes. A strip of carpet tacks around a pole, said to deter snakes, might work also for raccoons. Since raccoons perch on the roof when raiding a box, a strip of carpet tacks around the edge of the roof might be effective.

People have claimed success with any of a variety of predator guards made from sheet metal. For boxes mounted on wooden posts, wrap a piece at least a yard long around the post just beneath the box and make sure it extends a yard or more below the box. Pull it up firmly against the post, lap one end over the other, and nail it to the post. Unfortunately, raccoons have no difficulty climbing over this popular type of barrier (Curtis 1991). This structure, also often used beneath wood duck boxes, is simply not effective and not worth the effort to build.

For a box mounted on a pipe, get a piece of stove pipe at least two feet long. Cut a circle of wood to fit inside the stove pipe, and drill a hole in the center large enough to fit over your mounting pipe with about half an inch to spare. Tack the stove pipe onto the wooden piece, then slip the cylinder over your mounting pole. Let it rest just beneath where the box will be. You can keep it in place by wrapping tape around the pipe and over a couple of pieces of wood just beneath the cylinder to prevent it from sliding downward. The cylinder should fit loosely. A raccoon does not like to try to climb over something that is unstable.

Another type of predator guard is a sheet metal cone mounted on the pole beneath the bird house. Most predators are unable to get past such a structure. When made of thin aluminum, however, these structures are sometimes torn and destroyed by wind.

Raccoons, like all other animals, are lazy. The more difficult it is for a raccoon to get to your box, the less likely that he will succeed. Although a raccoon can easily climb a smooth plastic pipe, it will definitely prefer to go up a wooden post or a fence. Thus anything you do to make it less convenient to the raccoons the less likely that they will raid your boxes. Also, raccoons tend to forage along roads, paths, and fences; placing your boxes out and away from these, in the open field, will make them less vulnerable.

House Cats

Although house cats are notorious for preying on birds, they are not a major problem on the bluebird trail; problems with snakes and raccoons are much more frequent. Even at the University of Kentucky agricultural experiment farms, where at least one feral cat is resident in every barn, we usually have only one or two nests raided by cats in a season. Cat predation can usually be recognized by feathers of the young or adult bluebird beneath the box. Unlike snakes and raccoons, cats do not take eggs. A box raided by a cat does not have mud on the box and post as is usually left by a raccoon, and the cat does not leave traces of its fur. A cat usually messes up the nest but does not pull it out as the raccoon often does.

Cats are not nearly as adept at climbing as are snakes and raccoons. They can only climb a wooden post. They are, however, superb jumpers and can readily leap to a box five feet above the ground. Placing a box six feet or more above ground on a pipe will prevent predation by house cats. Boxes at these heights, however, become attractive to house sparrows and a person must balance one problem against the other. If you own a house cat and want to try to get bluebirds to nest in your yard, you should place the box out of reach of cats or build a predator guard. If you do not own a cat, it is probably best to place your boxes about four to five feet above ground.

Black Bears *(Ursus americanus)*

Where bears occur they can sometimes be destructive. Bob Stevenson in northeastern Minnesota reports that bears have continually devastated all his bluebird boxes. We know of no solution to the bear problem.

Squirrels and Chipmunks

Various kinds of squirrels can occasionally be problems at the bluebird box. The little red squirrel *(Tamiasciurus hudsonicus)* is the most carnivorous of our squirrels, well known for raiding birds nests and eating the young. Partial to evergreen forests, this northern species ranges southward in the higher mountains. Red squirrels will sometimes enlarge an opening and take up residence in boxes that are designed especially large and deep.

The little nocturnal flying squirrels *(Glaucomys volans* and *G. sabrinus)* enter nest boxes more frequently than any other squirrels. Although delightful animals, they can be destructive to bluebirds; they occasionally take over an active nest box and expel the bluebirds.

Our large tree squirrels, the gray squirrel *(Sciurus carolinensis)* and the fox squirrel *(S. niger)* are known to raid bird nests. (The fox squirrel is especially a threat to kestrels nesting in boxes placed for them.) Although tree squirrels will commonly chew on a bluebird nest box, enlarging the entrance and sometimes destroying the box, these squirrels are rarely, if ever, a threat to nesting bluebirds.

Our common chipmunk *(Tamias striatus)* and the various western species can and do climb trees and wooden poles. It is likely that they occasionally visit bluebird boxes, and they probably would eat young birds. I know of no reports of their destroying bluebird nests.

Any squirrel problem can usually be solved by not putting boxes on trees and by keeping boxes out of the woods. Except for boxes placed for western bluebirds, a tree should be the last resort as a place to mount a box.

Weasels

Several species of weasels live in the geographic range of bluebirds. All are carnivorous killers and will destroy any birds they encounter. They are not generally known for climbing ability, and I know of no instance of their raiding bluebird nests. In Europe, however, least weasels *(Mustela nivalis)* became serious predators in nest boxes placed on trees, raiding an average of 21 percent of the nests, rising as high as 50 percent in some years (Dunn 1977). Least weasels range throughout the northern states south to Kansas and Kentucky. These tiny animals could easily enter a bluebird box. Boxes mounted on any metal or plastic poles should be safe from weasels.

Red Fox *(Vulpes vulpes)*

Although our gray fox *(Urocyon cinereoargenteus)* can easily climb trees, the red fox is not known as a climber. Thus the report by Olson (1991) that a red fox had been leaping into boxes and destroying eggs and young is considered bizarre. We think bluebirders do not need to be concerned about foxes at the bluebird box.

Hawks and Other Birds

Several species of hawks have been known to capture bluebirds, but none is a common threat. The little kestrel *(Falco sparvarius)* is a cavity-nesting species. It will cling to the entrance of a bluebird box and would take young if it could reach them (Havera and Havera 1983; Wilkins 1992). Kestrels are fairly common residents in good bluebird habitat. They feed mainly on insects and mice but probably take a few bluebird fledglings on their first flight from the box. We find the two species usually in peaceful coexistence. The kestrel is a delightful native bird, much less common than bluebirds. People erect nesting boxes for kestrels; we should not be upset if they take an occasional bluebird.

Black Rat Snake   *American Kestral*

Pearman (1991) reported on a Swainson's hawk *(Buteo swainsoni)* that learned to anticipate fledging of bluebirds and capture them on their first flight. This common hawk of our western Great Plains might be a significant predator.

Pearman (1991) also reported that magpies *(Pica pica),* which occur only in western North America, learned to extract young bluebirds from nest boxes and that mortality became quite heavy. The magpies clung to a latch on the front of the boxes. Eliminating these perches solved the problem.

Hanert (1991) described a crow or a raven that perched on the roof of a bluebird box, reached into the entrance, extracted a young bluebird, and flew off with it. This was probably a rather unusual occurrence. The killing of a fledgling bluebird by a blue jay *(Cyanocitta cristata)* reported by Berner et al. (1992) was also an unusual event.

Predation in the box by large birds is generally a minor problem, if any, especially in comparison to predation by snakes and raccoons. You may want to consider the reports of such predation, however, if you intend to try some of the experimental house sparrow-inhibiting boxes that are shallow or have large entrances.

___ 10 ___
A Bluebird Trail

T HE IDEA OF A TRAIL of boxes designed to provide nesting opportunities for bluebirds apparently originated with T.E. Musselman of Quincy, Illinois. Dr. Musselman, a bird bander, combined his interest in bird migration with his concern about a decrease in the number of bluebirds. In 1934, he built twenty-five boxes, which he placed along the roads near his home in western Illinois. In the same year, he published an article entitled "Help the Bluebirds" in *Bird Lore,* as the magazine of the National Audubon Society was called at that time.

Musselman expanded his trail and wrote several papers on his bluebird studies. Based on his ideas, other bird banders adopted the

*A numbered box
with young
bluebirds*

practice of raising birds to band while helping to bring back the vanishing bluebird. Amelia Laskey in Nashville and Ralph Bell in southwestern Pennsylvania developed trails and banded bluebirds. As mentioned earlier, Bell secured permission from the power company to use their utility poles when he devised a method for hanging boxes in such a way that linemen can easily drop them to the ground when they need to climb the poles.

Along the Trans Canadian Highway through Manitoba and Saskatchewan runs the most remarkable bluebird trail in North America, established in 1959 by Dr. and Mrs. John Lane of Brandon, Manitoba. Today the trail, with numerous side branches, runs over twenty-five hundred miles, and dozens of people help to maintain it.

Zeleny (1976) gives a history of the concept of the bluebird trail and how the idea spread across the eastern United States and southern Canada. Since his book was published, the number of people involved in providing bluebird nest sites has grown exponentially. Developing and maintaining a bluebird trail has become a popular and delightful hobby for people of all ages. Soon after Zeleny's book was written, the North American Bluebird Society was established, and its membership continues to grow. Recently, many state bluebird societies have sprung up. All these organizations sponsor meetings at which bluebirders gather to discuss their experiences and problems with their bluebird trails.

Organizations, corporations, and government agencies now maintain bluebird trails. In Ohio, for example, the Dawes Arboretum and the Holden Arboretum each have substantial trails. The Dow Chemical Company plant at Granville, Ohio, maintains a trail of several dozen boxes on their grounds. This plan originated with employees and is supported by the administration; plans are underway for bluebird trails and other wildlife enhancement at other Dow plants.

The U.S. Army Corps of Engineers maintains bluebird trails at the recreational areas associated with Caesar Creek Reservoir in Ohio and at some of their other installations. By now, probably the majority of the state parks in most of our states have bluebird trails. Most of the organizations that have bluebird trails rely on volunteers to monitor and maintain the boxes.

*Checking boxes
by car*

Starting your own bluebird trail is easy. If you live in the country and have some land, put up some boxes first on your own land. If you are in a northern state where tree swallows breed, pair your boxes—one for the swallows and one for the bluebirds. If you live in the city, consider putting some boxes on the property of a friend or relative in a rural area. Nearly everyone who has adequate habitat will be receptive to the idea of having bluebird boxes.

If you have about a dozen boxes in good habitat, you can be reasonably confident of getting some bluebirds. After your initial success, you may want to expand your trail. Talk to the owners of the neighboring farm. Perhaps you can put some boxes on their fences along the road.

Most bluebird trails run along highways. In general, the fences along the major multilane highways are the property of the state highway departments, and fences along the two-lane roads belong to individual landowners.

If you put up boxes and abandon them, you may raise some bluebirds the first year. After that your trail will go downhill rapidly. Few of boxes are likely to have bluebirds the second year. Mice will pack some boxes so full of nesting material that a bluebird cannot enter. House wrens will do the same with their dry sticks. Bluebirds, unfortunately, usually do not remove materials from a nest box. House wrens and starlings will clean out a box and build nests to their liking, but bluebirds simply give up if they find a box filled with something.

An absolute requirement for raising bluebirds is that each box be visited once a year. Check all boxes in late winter and ask the deer mice to vacate for the coming season. Old bluebird nests that have fledged young the previous year (a firm, flattened nest containing droppings) should be left to help control blowfly parasites. The bluebirds will build their new nest upon it, actually preferring that site to an empty box.

Such a protocol will assure that you raise some bluebirds each year. With this schedule, however, you will probably not get many second broods. Ants may move in and take over many boxes, and various other problems can becloud your efforts. Since the first broods often succumb to rain and cool weather, second broods are usually more productive—if you monitor your trail and care for your birds. The best procedure is to regularly monitor all the boxes on your trail throughout the nesting season.

You can check your boxes as often as you like. Some people check them daily. Bluebirds are remarkably tolerant of people looking in on them. Most trail operators try to check their boxes weekly; such a schedule will allow you to take care of most problems that arise and will assure you of fledging a large number of bluebirds.

If you plan to establish a bluebird trail, one of your first decisions is whether to buy or build boxes. If you choose to buy boxes, remember that many on the market are unsatisfactory; you must be discriminating. Never buy a box that is made of a material that seems likely to overheat, and always make sure the box is designed to provide adequate ventilation. Buy boxes with your sites in mind; you may choose one design for a box you plan to mount high on a pole

*Don't hesitate
to open a box.*

and another for one you'll erect only three feet from the ground. Never buy a box that can't be opened; you won't be able to check on your birds, and as soon as a mouse or another bird moves in or a colony of ants finds the box, it becomes useless. Wild Birds Unlimited carries an assortment of acceptable boxes. You might try to interest your local Audubon Society, 4-H club, or scout troop in building and selling suitable boxes.

For a trail of any significant length, buying boxes becomes expensive. Nearly all individual trail operators build their own. With a minimum of carpentry skills, you can construct boxes bluebirds will be happy to inhabit. For instructions on nest box construction, see chapter 11.

As your trail grows to beyond a few boxes, you will find it helpful to number them. Some people use a grease pencil or a felt-tipped

Monitoring the trail

permanent marker. A mark inside the box, away from weather damage, will last longer. Some people number boxes with paint, either with a brush or using stencils and a spray can. Others prefer a metal tag, such as those used for nursery stock. You can make your own tags from a piece of sheet aluminum gutter material. Most people put the tags on the boxes, but others prefer to tag the post; boxes may be removed for repair or replaced.

You will want to make note of the location of each box so that you can find it easily. For some areas, a map may be necessary. If your boxes are along a road and you check them by automobile, an alternative to numbering is to record the mileage at each box. This method has the advantage that adding or deleting a box does not cause confusion.

You should keep records of every visit to each box. Compare the conditions you find on the present visit with the record of your visit the previous week. If, for example, you find three eggs in a box, it is important to know that there were five last week. Without this information, you would never suspect that a snake had raided the box and that a new clutch had been started. By keeping good records, you will be more able to recognize problems of predation and take appropriate action.

Do not hesitate to look into a box that is being used by bluebirds. They are remarkably tolerant and will not abandon the box because of your attention. If the female is on the nest she will usually fly away as you approach. If she does, check the nest quickly and move on so she can return. Sometimes the female will remain on the nest when you open the box. If this happens, quietly close the box and record that she is on the nest. She may be laying an egg. Some people recommend that you avoid checking boxes in the morning because that is apparently when laying occurs. Often when the female remains on the nest, she will leave the box as you walk away; you can then go back and check the nest.

When there are young in a nest, check for blowfly larvae. If these parasites are abundant they can weaken the young and occasionally kill them. In some areas and in some years they can become a major problem, although usually their effect is not significant. A dozen or so are usually considered harmless, while fifty or more may be a problem. For further discussion of blowflies and bluebirds, see chapter 7, Pests and Guests.

Some trail monitors routinely remove any nest with young and shake it gently. Most of the blowfly larvae will fall out of the nesting material onto the ground; the nest and the young are then replaced. Other trail monitors routinely remove nest and young, replace the old nest with dry grass, place the young in the new nest material, and discard the old nest. This may seem like a drastic action, but it is readily accepted by the parents.

If your boxes are not protected from crawling ants, check each nest for them. Usually the ants swarm out when the box is opened. Sometimes, however, a small colony may not be readily evident. It is a good idea to slide a screwdriver along the edges of the floor beneath the nest; this will cause ants to appear if they are present.

Several writers have repeated Zeleny's (1976) warning that you should not monitor a box after the young are twelve days old lest they fledge prematurely when unable to fly and become easy prey for predators. Banders occasionally have a problem of the young not wanting to stay in the box after they have been removed and handled, but if you are careful you can safely check the box and the young will not leave unless they are ready to fledge. When you open a box, the young will scrunch down and grasp the nest material with their feet. If you try to remove one, it will strongly resist.

You should continue to monitor a box right up until the young are ready to fledge. The likelihood that you will save bluebirds by discovering problems at a manageable stage is greater than the likelihood that you will lose birds to premature fledging. I once opened a box to find two large young standing on two dead and rotting siblings. I removed the dead young and placed some dry grass beneath the living ones. Three days later they fledged.

The occasional bird that takes flight when you open a box is ready to leave. It will fly to a tree or other nearby perch, where the parents are likely to find it. Of course, it is better that the young leave a box with their parents coaxing them out. If you approach a box and see young birds looking out the entrance, leave them undisturbed and simply record that they are near fledging.

There has been concern in recent years that human visitation at the nest may attract predators, that a raccoon may follow the human trail and visit every box. This idea gained wide credence as a result of a study by Bart (1977) that suggested that predation was heavier on nests visited by people than on those that were not. A later analysis (Bart and Robson 1982), however, indicated that the previous study may have involved a misinterpretation of the data. Nichols et al. (1984) reviewed the numerous studies on the subject and found no evidence that human visits attract predators and no difference in nesting success between birds visited daily and those visited weekly. Major (1990), in a study in New Zealand, reported nest predation heavier when nests were visited by people, though this study involved small samples with marginal significance. Martin and Roper (1988) found that the number of visits by people to nests was not related to nesting success or failure.

The number of visits you make to your boxes will probably not have any effect on predation rate. An exception may be if you beat a path through weeds. Foraging mammals tend to travel the easiest paths, and a beaten path might induce a raccoon to explore where it otherwise would not.

After the young have fledged, you will find the old nest flattened from the weight of the fledglings and often fouled with droppings, dead June beetles, and wild cherry seeds. Although most trail monitors remove and carry off all old nests as soon as the young have fledged, you should not disturb the old nest. Darling and Thomson-Delaney (1993) found that the minute wasps that are parasitic on the blowflies build up their population through the summer and are important in controlling the population of these blood-sucking parasites that attack nestling bluebirds. Your bluebirds will readily build their next nest on the old one.

Your visits to the boxes on your trail should be a pleasant aspect of your hobby. This is the opportunity to observe the success of your efforts. When you open a box, the shy youngsters will scrunch down into their nest and look at you with expressions of fright and bewilderment. You close the box and move on, thinking about the little fellows: if you hadn't put the box there, they would never have been born.

11

Building Your Own

NEARLY ALL PEOPLE who operate bluebird trails build their own boxes. They are easy to make and require a minimum of skill and few tools. With the following designs and instructions, you'll be able to construct boxes, feeders, and predator guards sturdier and more favorable to bluebirds than any you can purchase.

Tools

A good slot entrance box can be built with standard soft pine lumber using only a saw, a hammer, a ruler, and a few galvanized nails. If this is the limit of your tool chest and you plan to make only a couple of boxes, go to it. Your boxes will attract bluebirds and will last several years.

If you are a little more serious about building boxes, your next most important tool is a power drill. A drill is handy for mounting boxes, and it will allow you to use sturdier, more durable wood, such as oak, for your boxes. You can predrill nail holes, which will make assembling your box easier and will prevent splits in the wood. Even if nondrilled wood does not split upon assembly, it tends to split with weathering, so a drill will add life to your boxes.

You may also want to replace your hand saw with a power tool. An electric circular saw will permit you to make cuts quickly and easily, and building a dozen or so boxes becomes a reasonable chore. If you plan to build a large number of boxes, you may want to invest in a table saw. This tool will put a small sawmill into your workshop. Rip cuts and cross cuts can be made rapidly and accurately, and you can quickly cut and stack all the pieces you need for making a number of boxes. You don't need standard lumber sizes; you can use any

Building a box takes a minimum of tools and materials.

kind of scrap and cut it to the sizes you want. Although a table saw is expensive, you can recover part of the cost by selling boxes. The boxes you build will be better than those commercially available.

Materials

Almost any kind of lumber can be used for birdhouses, though there are some tradeoffs. Cedar, cypress, redwood, and hemlock resist weathering, but they also tend to split and may be easily destroyed by vandals. Treated lumber, which is often used for outdoor decks, does not decay with weathering or even in contact with the ground; it is, however, pressure-treated with chromium, copper, and arsenic (CCA), a mixture of elements toxic to all life. Bacteria, fungi, and insects, usually responsible for the decay of wood, will not attack it.

We do not know if treated lumber is harmful to birds, but it probably is not. Because CCA consists of heavy metals that have a low volatility, their primary danger would be to an animal that eats the wood.

When I have treated lumber scraps, I use it for floors, because they are usually the first part of a box to decay. I have experimented with treated lumber, thinking that it would deter ants because those we have chew up the wood to make a paperlike material called carton. Unfortunately, however, ants *do* invade boxes that contain treated lumber.

Treated lumber is much more of a threat to the builder than to the bluebirds. Anytime you operate your table saw you should wear a dust mask to minimize the inhalation of the fine sawdust; but treated lumber is too dangerous to cut on a table saw. I run an extension cord outdoors and cut the lumber with my circular saw. I avoid breathing any dust. Arsenic is quite toxic to people. It is probably best to avoid using treated lumber at all.

Plywood is good material for nest boxes. When plywood or particle board is used, drywall screws should be the fasteners of choice; corrugated underlayment nails and galvanized nails are also satisfactory. Common nails will not hold.

If you want a material that will last indefinitely, you might consider using Rivenite, a lumber substitute designed for outdoor use. It is made from recycled plastics and is being used for outdoor benches, tables, and decks. It will not split and does not decay but otherwise behaves quite like lumber.

If you plan to build many boxes, consider scrounging lumber instead of buying it. You'll save money and you won't be contributing to the destruction of the forests as you do when you buy wood. Also, while scrounging wood you may stimulate the interest of other people in bluebirds.

Scrap lumber is generated and destroyed almost daily in almost every community, and with a bit of looking you will probably be able to find more than you can use. Home builders generate scrap, which they burn or have hauled to the dump. Your local landfill operator may be willing to help. Some lumber companies have a scrap pile that they may make available to you, as well as warped and damaged unsalable pieces. Grape cartons from the supermarket and packing crates from retailers of office and household furniture and appliances can provide waste lumber suitable for bluebird boxes. You will find most people glad to help your cause and glad for your help with their trash disposal. Since such small cuts are used to assemble bird houses, even the most severely warped pieces of lumber can be used. I have built thousands of bluebird houses and have never bought a piece of lumber for that purpose.

Painting your wooden boxes will prolong their life. You should probably choose an exterior latex. Almost any color will do. Brown, gray, and green are popular. Avoid black because a black box tends to overheat. White, of course, reflects the most light and thus provides the coolest box. Hobart Ellifritt of Clarksburg, West Virginia, paints his boxes with a wide variety of colors and has bluebirds using all shades. He is a district representative for a paint company, and as a hobby he makes and puts up hundreds of boxes.

Choosing Designs

Numerous styles and modifications of bluebird boxes have been developed by many different people. All have their advantages and disadvantages, which should be of little concern to the beginner. Any of the styles of boxes described here will attract bluebirds, so you should pick whichever ones take your fancy to start your trail. Certain generalizations, however, apply to any box design.

Openings

Boxes may be built to open from the top, the sides, or the front. The one absolute rule that applies to any style box you build is that *you must be able to open it*. A box that is nailed shut is almost worthless. It may raise a brood or two the first year, but after that it will likely become filled with material brought in by various birds and other animal life and bluebirds will refuse to use it. We prefer a front opening hinged at the bottom far enough below an inset floor so that it flops down completely. This allows for easy observation and ease of cleaning.

Several veteran bluebirders prefer a top opening. The advantage is the ease of counting eggs and young. Some people fear that a front opening box will cause nest or young to come out, but this fear is unjustified. A disadvantage of the top-opening design is the difficulty of cleaning. Harry Krueger solved this problem by hinging his floor with a pair of nails near the back and securing the floor with a single screw through the front. Don Wilkins mounts his top opening boxes on a swivel so that he can invert them for cleaning.

We have found that the simplest and best closing method is a single finishing nail driven part way into a side piece and bent over the front. It can easily be pushed aside to open the box and just as easily returned to close it. We have found the very common method of drilling a downward slanting hole through the side and into the front and sticking nail in to hold the front closed is less satisfactory. The nail will rust and bind unless the hole is considerably larger than the nail, in which case the nail tends to get lost. Also, with weathering it becomes more difficult to match up the holes when trying to close the box.

If your boxes are to be in a place where people are likely to cause problems, such as a public park, neither of the above closing methods will be satisfactory. In this case it is best to close your box with a screw run through the side and into the front piece. Harry Krueger suggests using a lead anchor. Otherwise, with repeated opening, the wood holding the screw wears away. You will need a screwdriver to open the box and most people will not recognize that it can be opened at all.

Another important consideration is that any box must provide proper ventilation. Your boxes will be placed in the open usually in full sunlight and, although bluebirds are quite tolerant of heat, young can be killed by very hot weather if your box is not ventilated. Any box with a standard circular entrance 1½ inches in diameter should be ventilated by leaving a half-inch slot beneath the roof, either on both sides or in front and back. A slot entrance box can be ventilated by leaving a slot of a quarter to a half inch at the back beneath the roof. You can also improve the ventilation of a box by knocking off the corners of your floor. In all except our northernmost states, bluebirds occur in winter and spend cold nights in boxes; ventilation slots make boxes less suitable in winter. Richard Tuttle in Ohio plugs all ventilation holes in the fall and opens them when hot weather arrives.

Nearly all writings on bluebird trail management stress a need to provide for drainage, either by drilling holes in the floor or by knocking off about a quarter inch on each of the four corners. I have never built a box that would hold water and have seen no need to provide drainage. Drainage spaces will do no harm, however, and they may improve ventilation.

Roofs

The roof is the most vulnerable part of a box. All other pieces are tied in with nails or screws in more than one direction. If you simply nail the roof into place, it is likely to come off within a year or so. After a little weathering loosens it, a wind storm will simply pick it up. You should fasten the roof with wood screws or drywall screws. If nails are used, try specialty nails such as spiraled nails, underlayment nails, or sinker nails. Slanting your nails will provide a better hold. Put two nails through the roof into a side, slanting them in opposite directions. You may also enhance the roof fasteners by wiring the roof to the sides of the box.

You may want to consider especially large roofs. When raccoons raid boxes, they perch on the roof. Berner et al. (1990) found that a roof extended seven inches inhibits raccoons. For a slot entrance box you may want to extend the roof beyond the sides as well. Extended roofs also have the advantage of better protection from weather.

You might also consider making a drip protector on the underside of your roof. About an inch back from what will be the front edge of your roof take a saw and cut a slight groove across what will be the underside. During a storm water droplets will adhere to the underside of a flat roof and wind can push them inside. The groove will prevent this.

Floors

Another good generalization for nest boxes is that the floor should be inset rather than nailed onto the bottom. We have built many boxes of both styles and found the former definitely preferable, although it requires slightly more lumber. With a floor nailed to the bottom, water will find its way in. Nests get wet, the floor rots, and eventually the bottom of the sides and back rot and the floor falls off. With the floor inset an inch or so, your boxes will last much longer.

The size of the floor and thus the internal dimensions of your box is an important consideration. Bluebirds do not like a large floor area. Our choice of floor size is 4 x 4 inches, but we find 3½ x 4 inches perfectly satisfactory. Many experienced trail operators prefer a slightly larger box of 4¼ or 4½ inches.

Entrances

There are two major styles of bluebird boxes—those with a circular entrance and those with a slot entrance. Each has its advantages and disadvantages.

A circular entrance box has an entrance hole 1½ inches in diameter (1⁹⁄₁₆ for mountain bluebirds, which are a little larger than the other two species). Such a box has long been the standard. It is readily accepted by bluebirds, and it looks more like a bird house than does a slot entrance box. Its main advantage is that it can accept the various predator exclusion devices and house sparrow traps that the slot entrance box cannot.

The slot entrance box has an entrance formed by letting the front come to within 1⅛ inches (28 to 30 mm) of the flat roof. The box is a simple design and easy to build. When we paired them with standard boxes, bluebirds selected the slot boxes 70 percent of the time (McComb et al. 1987). Richard Tuttle found that bluebirds chose his slot boxes in 80 percent of his paired-box tests, while tree swallows chose the standard boxes. When we alternated the styles on a trail, bluebirds used more of the slot entrance type and left many standard boxes empty (Davis 1991). House sparrows, on the other hand, showed a strong preference for the circular entrance (Davis 1989b).

Other advantages of the slot box are that a predator or house sparrow cannot easily close off an escape route for an adult bluebird it has trapped in a box, a sparrow cannot as easily exclude nesting bluebirds by sitting in the box with his beak in an entrance hole, and when young are near fledging one cannot take exclusive possession of the entrance and monopolize feeding opportunities. The slot entrance provides better ventilation than a circular one. Finally, the fact that a slot entrance box is not readily recognized as a bird house by people may deter vandalism. Hobart Ellifritt, who builds elegant standard boxes to place along the highways in West Virginia, loses many of them to theft and vandalism, whereas I seldom lose boxes.

Results of our experiments at the University of Kentucky have so consistently shown the superiority of the slot entrance that we have quit making circular entrance boxes and we use a slot entrance box as the standard against which we test new designs. Tests conducted in Iowa and New York did not confirm our results, however; slot entrance boxes did not perform as well as other styles. In their tests Berner and Pleines (1993) found the Peterson box performed better than either standard or slot entrance boxes. Therefore, in addition to slot entrance boxes we will provide designs for the Peterson and a standard box.

Building Boxes, Feeders, Traps, and Guards

After you have chosen your design, gather the materials and tools necessary and follow the simple instructions provided. Remember that some traps and predator guards will fit only on certain kinds of boxes and choose your designs accordingly.

Paper milk carton box

Use a paper half-gallon milk carton. Cut a hole 1½ inches in diameter about one inch below the top on the side away from where the carton was opened. Paint the carton with two coats of a gray or brown outdoor latex paint. Fasten it to a post by putting nails through the "ears" formed when the carton was opened and by toeing nails in through the floor and the back. Cut two or three small holes in the floor for drainage. Such a nest box will last one and sometimes two seasons.

Gallon jug box

Another simple nest structure can be made from plastic gallon jugs of the type that are used as containers for vinegar, bleach, windshield washer, antifreeze, and several other products. Clean the container thoroughly, cut an entrance opposite the handle, and paint with two coats of gray or brown exterior latex. Throw away the lid. As over-heating is a problem with plastic structures, the ventilation at the top is much more important than preventing the small amount of rain that will enter. Cut a horizontal slit about two to three inches wide and a quarter inch high just below the handle to improve ventilation. Drill four holes about one-quarter inch in diameter in the floor for drainage and two such holes at the back near the bottom for mounting. Extend one of these as a slot similar to the one above to improve ventilation.

Mount your jug on a steel fence post with a wire around the handle and one through the holes near the bottom. As wires tend to cut through the plastic with time and weathering, insulated electric wire used for the bottom fastener will improve the life of the jug. Jugs can last for many years but tend to become brittle and break easily after three years.

A good, standard bluebird box

In January 1993, the now-defunct *Bluebird News* of Mount Pleasant, Texas, published plans for a good, standard bluebird box. With a hammer and a saw, scrap wood, and a few nails, you can build this box in an hour or two. It is simple enough for even beginning builders.

Tools. You will need a hammer and a saw. A drill is helpful.

Materials. You will need standard one-by-five and one-by-seven lumber and a few nails.

Directions. Cut two sides 10 x 4¾ inches; a back 15½ x 6¼ inches; a front 10½ x 6¼ inches; a floor 4¾ x 4¾ inches; and a roof 8 x 9 inches. Cut an entrance hole in the front piece precisely 1½ inches in diameter 1¼ inches from the top edge of the front of the box. Attach one side to the back so that the top edge is 2¾ inches down from the top of the back piece. Attach the other side with one 1¾-inch galvanized nail through the back piece and into the side. Do not nail the pivot side. Align the bottom of the front piece with the bottoms of the side pieces, and attach the front to the first side with nails. Drive a second

Figure 1. A good, standard bluebird box

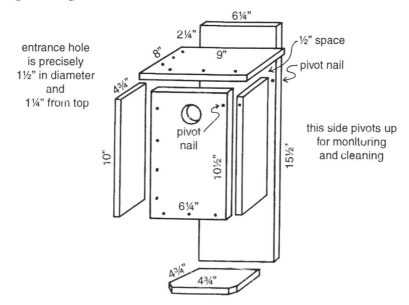

nail through the front and into the pivoting side. Cut three-eights of an inch off the corners of the floor for drainage and attach the floor, recessing it one-quarter inch. Attach the flat roof 2¼ inches down from the top of the back piece, which will allow one-half inch between the top of each side piece and the roof for ventilation.

Kentucky bluebird box

This box is simple to build and requires a minimum of tools. It has an advantage in that all pieces fit together perfectly without any rip cutting needed.

Tools. To make this box, you can get by with a hammer, a saw, a drill, and a ruler. If you have a table saw and plan to make many boxes, you will save time and effort by making a block for measuring the height of your slot entrance. Such a block is more convenient than measuring with a ruler. Shave a piece of two-by-four with your table saw until it is 28 mm thick. A drill is helpful but not necessary for building this box.

*Author Davis
with a Kentucky
Bluebird Box*

Materials. You will need three eight-inch pieces of one-by-six for sides
and roof; two seven-inch pieces of one-by-four for the front and back,
and one four-inch piece of one-by-four for the floor; if your lumber is
warped, cut a piece of plywood for the roof. You will also need a
dozen number 5d galvanized nails and a 6d finishing nail.

Directions. Drill through one side and into the back and nail. Repeat
on the other side. Position the floor in place against the back and inset

Figure 2. The Kentucky bluebird box

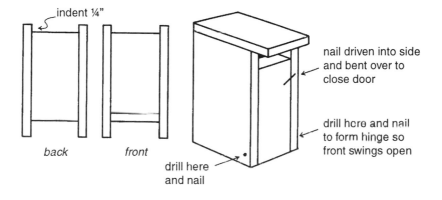

it an inch from the bottom; drill and nail into place. The disadvantage of this box is that the thin floor may give you problems. When nailing it into place, you may split it or even miss it entirely with your nails. You can avoid this problem by using a piece of two-by-four for the floor.

Drill the roof and nail it into place or fasten it with drywall screws. If you do not have a drill, you will need to arrange for mounting your box when you put the roof on. Take a piece of soft wire long enough to go around the post you wish to mount it on and lay it across the top of the sides near the back. When you put on the roof, nail it into the sides just behind the wire. After checking to be sure that the front will fit into place, nail down the roof.

Position the front piece so that its top edge is within 1⅛ inches (28 to 30 mm) of the roof. (This forms the slot for the birds to enter and exit.) Drill through one side a half inch above its lower edge and into the edge of the front; nail in place. Repeat on the other side.

For a closure, drive a finishing nail halfway into the edge of one side and bend it over to hold the front in place. The nail can be pushed aside to open the box.

Check your measurements. The slot opening must be at least 28 mm at some point and no more than 30 mm at any point. Slight errors can be corrected by tapping with a hammer.

Gilbertson's sparrow-inhibiting nest box

In our experiments at the University of Kentucky we found that the PVC box developed by Steve Gilbertson is the best of the various sparrow-inhibiting boxes. Bluebirds liked them, and few of them were used by house sparrows (Davis and Mack 1994). A bonus is that they present a challenge to raccoons and house cats. They are easy to build and we recommend that bluebirders try them. The following plan is slightly modified from Gilbertson (1991; 1993).

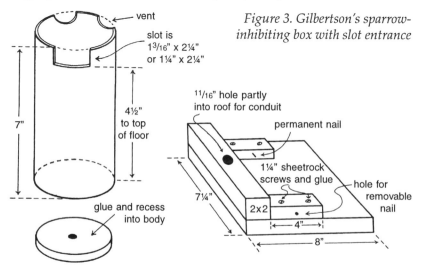

Figure 3. Gilbertson's sparrow-inhibiting box with slot entrance

Tools. You will need a drill and ⅛-, ¹¹/₁₆-, and ³/₃₂-inch bits; a hacksaw or a table saw; a power emery wheel, jig saw, coping saw, or a 4¼-inch circular hole saw with a drill press; pliers; and a hammer.

Materials. You will need two four-inch side pieces cut from a one-by-two; an eight-inch section of one-by-eight for the roof; a 7¼-inch section of two-by-two; a circle of wood four inches in diameter; a seven-inch section of PVC pipe four inches in diameter; 6d and 10d finishing nails; 1½-inch sheet rock or drywall screws; construction adhesive or small nails; and brown, gray, or green exterior latex paint. (If you are able to buy gray pipe, you will not need to paint.) Gilbertson recommends that the inside be painted dark.

If you plan to mount the box on a wooden or steel post, you will need a forty-inch piece of half-inch metal conduit. For mounting without a post, you will need a five-foot piece of half-inch metal conduit, a five-foot piece of half-inch concrete reinforcement bar (rebar), a conduit connector, and a bolt at least a half inch long to replace the bottom one of the two supplied with the connector.

Directions. On the seven-inch piece of PVC pipe, mark the slot entrance 28 mm down from the top edge and two inches wide. Cut out the opening with a powered emery wheel. Cut two ventilation openings opposite the slot entrance. If you have a drill press and a 1½-inch circular hole saw you can cut these openings as half circles. Paint both the inside and the outside of the pipe, if necessary.

For the floor, cut circular piece of wood 4 inches in diameter. The easiest way to get a piece this size is to use a 4¼-inch circular hole saw in a drill press. The piece will be 4 inches in diameter. The arbor makes a neat drainage hole in the center. The option is to mark off a circle with a compass and cut it out with your jig saw or coping saw. Drill one or more drainage holes in the floor. Position the floor so that it is 4½ inches below the lower edge of the entrance. Fasten it in place with construction adhesive or drill with your small bit and secure it in place with small nails or screws.

For the roof, drill through the two-by-two section with the ¹¹/₁₆-inch bit, then fasten this piece with screws to the one-by-eight section. Turn the roof over, position the side pieces against the back piece, and fit up against the PVC piece. Drill and fasten side pieces to the roof. Turn the roof on its side and, at the midpoint of one side piece, drill a hole with the ³/₃₂-inch bit, angling downward. Put the PVC piece into place and drill into it. Enlarge this hole so that a 6d finishing nail will fit into it. Carefully drive a 6d nail through the hole in the side piece until about a quarter-inch of the nail end protrudes on the inside, where it should catch and hold the PVC piece. From the center of the other side, drill through with the ⅛-inch bit, also slanting downward and into the PVC piece. Grip the head of a 10d finishing nail with the pliers, bend a half inch of it at a ninety degree angle. Put the nail through the hole into the PVC piece to hold the body firmly in place.

It can easily be removed for checking and cleaning by simply slipping the bent nail partway out.

To mount your Gilbertson sparrow-inhibiting box on a fence post, cut a forty-inch piece of conduit using a pipe cutter or a hack saw. Fit one end of the conduit into the back piece of the roof. Drill through the back piece into the conduit and fasten with a screw. Drill two holes through the other end of the conduit about six inches apart. Nail or screw the conduit support to a wooden post or wire it to a steel post.

To mount your box where no post is available, drive a five-foot piece of half-inch rebar halfway into the ground. Mount your box on a five-foot piece of conduit, shove the conduit down over the rebar, and secure it with a conduit connector.

You may easily adapt the Gilbertson box to a circular entrance style by cutting the PVC pieces eight inches long and drilling a 1½-inch entrance hole three-quarters of an inch below the top. You may also discourage raccoon predation by polishing your conduit mounting pieces with coarse steel wool.

Figure 4. Gilbertson's sparrow-inhibiting box with circular entrance

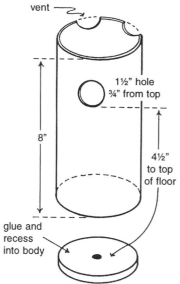

vent

1½" hole ¾" from top

8"

4½" to top of floor

glue and recess into body

Zuern's horizontal box

A new idea on protection from raccoons and cats has been developed by Frank Zuern of Wisconsin. He has developed a horizontal box designed so that the bluebirds nest beyond the reach of the predator. Testing over several years by people in Wisconsin has been encouraging. In an experiment in Kentucky we also found that this box provided protection from raccoons (Davis and Kalisz 1995). The follow-

ing is our modification and simplification of Zuern's design as we
developed it when building several dozen for testing in Kentucky.

Tools. You will need a drill with ³/₃₂-, ⁷/₆₄-, and 1½-inch bits; a hammer; and a saw.

Materials. You will need sections of one-by-four: one piece five inches
long for the front, one piece 5¼ inches long for the back, two pieces
16½ inches long, one for the floor and one for the mounting board,

Figure 5. Zeurn's horizontal box

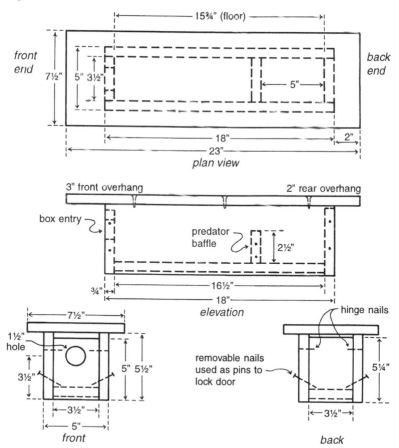

and a baffle 2½ x 3½ inches, which you can cut by making a rip cut or by splitting off an inch with a hammer and a chisel or screwdriver. You will also need two pieces of one-by-six eighteen inches long for the sides, and a piece of one-by-eight twenty-three inches long for the roof. You will also need 4d and 6d galvanized nails.

Directions. Set your mounting board at the midpoint of one side piece, perpendicular with it and with an end even with the edge of the side piece. Nail the mounting piece firmly into place with 4d nails. (You may want to use wood screws or drywall screws instead.) With the sides extending three-quarters of an inch beyond the floor on both ends and with the mounting board pointing downward, drill and nail the sides to the floor using 6d nails or screws. Set the baffle into place on the floor five inches from one end (this end will be the back of the box). Drill with your small bit and nail into place with 4d nails. Put the back piece into place in such a way that there will be a quarter-inch ventilation slot beneath the roof. With your small bit, drill through the side an inch below the top so as to strike the edge of the back piece. Nail with a 4d nail. Repeat on the other side, thus making a hinge so that the back can be opened for inspection by swinging up from the bottom. Then with your larger bit an inch or two from the bottom drill through the sides on a downward sloping angle and well into the back piece. Stick 6d nails into these holes to hold the back in place. The nails may be lifted out to open the box for inspection. Raccoons are clever animals. If you think they might pull out these nails, you can add to your security system by driving 6d finishing nails halfway into the side boards and bending them over the back piece. They can be pushed aside to open the back. An alternative is to fasten the back with a screw.

Set the front into place. There should be a half-inch space above it for ventilation. Make a hinge and closures as you did with the back. Put the roof into place. If you plan to mount your box on a post so that it sticks up above the post, you can center the roof. If, however, you plan to mount your box on a utility pole, on the side of a building, or on a tree (the least favored spot for any bluebird box), you should offset your roof so that one edge coincides with the outer edge of the mounting board. Drill through the roof and nail firmly to the sides with 6d nails, or use screws. You should also nail the roof to the top edge of the mounting board and perhaps nail the mounting board through to the floor with 6d nails. Raccoons are large, powerful, and persistent, so your box should be of sturdy construction.

To mount your box, drill holes through the mounting board with your larger bit and nail firmly to your mounting post with 8d nails or sturdy wood screws.

Zuern says that bluebirds always nest beyond the baffle, where they cannot be reached by raccoons or house cats. In our tests we found that only 20 percent of the nests were in front of the baffle where the raccoons were able to destroy them; all other nestings were successful (Davis and Kalisz 1995). Zuern's design includes numerous holes drilled through the floor and through the sides just beneath the roof for drainage and to increase ventilation.

Peterson box

This box, designed by Richard Peterson of Minneapolis, has several unique features that apparently make it attractive to bluebirds. Tests by Kevin Berner in New York and by us in Kentucky have shown that, when given a choice, bluebirds show a definite preference for a Peterson box compared to other style boxes. A disadvantage is that the size of the entrance makes this box readily accessible to starlings. Although starlings will rarely nest in the box, evidence suggests that they occasionally disrupt the bluebirds.

Tools. You will need a hammer, a saw, a drill, and a ¾-inch and a 1⅜-inch bit.

Materials. You will need to carefully cut a piece of ¾-inch plywood to match the measurements on figure 6. You will also need nail

Directions. To build a Peterson box, measure carefully. Make th trance by drilling two holes and taking out the extra wood or sides with a wood chisel. Lay the back piece and the roof sup piece into position and nail a side onto them. Turn the pieces c and attach the other side.

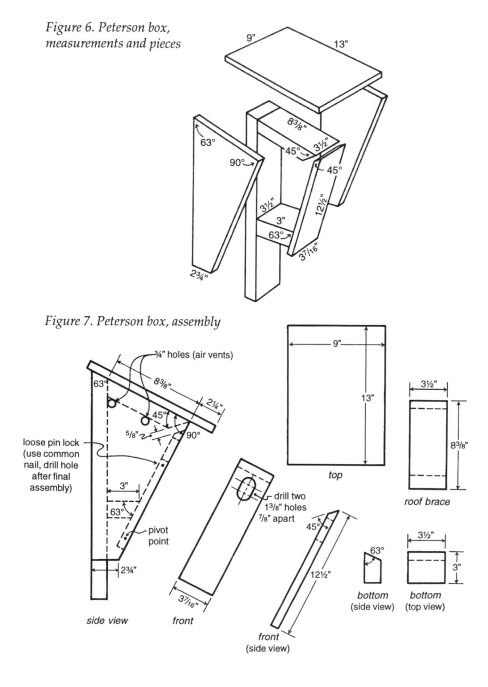

Figure 6. Peterson box, measurements and pieces

Figure 7. Peterson box, assembly

Put the floor into position so that its surface is perpendicular to the back and so that there is room for the front piece to fit up against it. Put the front into place in such a way as to leave a half inch or so ventilation space between the front and the roof support piece. With the front piece firmly up against the floor, put a hinge nail through the side and into the front piece, locating the nail about halfway between the bottom of the floor and the bottom of the side piece. Drilling through the side with a bit the size of the hinge nail will ease this task. Turn the box over and put in the hinge nail on the other side. Fasten the roof onto the roof support piece with nails or screws. Finally, using a drill bit larger than your closing nail, drill through a side at a downward angle into the front piece near the top of the front piece and stick the nail in to hold the front in place. An alternative is to drive a 6d finishing nail halfway into a side and bend it over the front for a closure.

A Bluebird Feeder

The size of feeder you build will depend on the materials you have on hand. The ideal size is approximately twelve inches long, but the design may be adapted to available materials.

Figure 8. Bluebird feeder

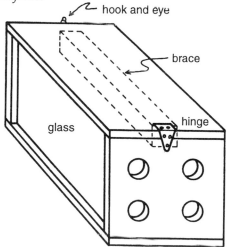

Tools. You will need an electric saw, table saw, hand saw, or router; a hammer; and a drill.

Materials. You will need two pieces of Plexiglas (ideally, approximately 12 x 6 inches); two end pieces of one-by-ten, each as long as the width of the Plexiglas; two pieces of one-by-ten, each slightly longer than the length of the Plexiglas, for floor and roof; a 12-inch piece of two-by-two for a brace. If you plan to bolt the feeder to the platform, you will need two quarter-inch bolts 2¼ inches long and two nuts and four washers to fit the bolts.

Directions. With an electric saw, a table saw, or a router set to cut a depth of a quarter of an inch, cut grooves about an inch from each edge of what will be the inner faces of the end pieces. (These can be cut with a handsaw if necessary.) The Plexiglas sides are to fit into these grooves. Drill two or more entrance holes 1½ inches in diameter into each end piece. Make at least two of these holes close to the bottom; this makes it easier for the birds to find their way in and out on their first encounter with your feeder.

Hold one end piece at a right angle to the floor with the grooves toward the inside. Drill through the floor and into the end piece and fasten with two-inch wood screws, drywall screws, or number 6d nails. Fasten the other end piece the same way, and slide the Plexiglas sides into place. Carefully measure the inside distance across the top from one end piece to the other and cut a two-by-two to this length. Fit the two-by-two between the two end pieces and fasten firmly with screws or nails, forming a brace to hold the ends in position.

The roof, a piece identical to the floor, is fastened on one end with two small hinges. On the other end, a hook and eye allow the roof to be lifted easily.

There are two good ways of mounting your feeder. Whichever method you choose, you will not mount your feeder directly on the pole or post. As explained in chapter 6, Bluebirds at Your Feeder, you need to start with a platform feeder and train your bluebirds to use it. Your platform should be about eight inches longer than your feeder, giving the bluebirds porches on either end where they can feed and eventually learn to enter the feeder. The platform can be made of the same lumber as the feeder or of three-quarter-inch plywood.

You may use a threaded iron pipe and a floor plate as described in the section on building out raccoons in this chapter. This mounting has the advantage of being easily moveable. Another method is to get a treated wooden fence post at your farm supply dealer and mount your platform on the top of the post using three or four angle irons.

When you are ready to mount your feeder onto the platform, simply position the feeder where you want it, drill through the platform and the floor of the feeder, and use the bolts to secure it.

Huber sparrow trap

Among bluebirders, the best known trap for house sparrows is the Huber trap, which captures a sparrow when it enters a box. It is rather easy to build or may be purchased from various commercial outlets, such as Wild Birds Unlimited, or from Joe Huber himself. See the Appendix for information on how to order directly from the inventor.

Figure 9.
Huber sparrow trap

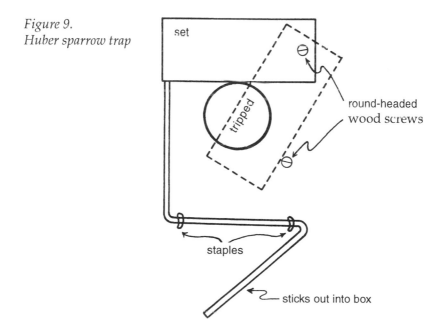

set

tripped

round-headed
wood screws

staples

sticks out into box

Figure 10. Huber's flip flop front box

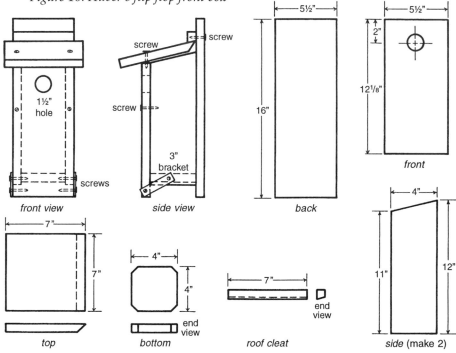

To make a Huber sparrow trap, drill a 1½-inch entrance hole in the piece of wood similar to the front of your nest box. For the trap, Joe Huber uses a piece of sheet steel, which he gets at a hardware store. We have found that a piece of Plexiglas serves well. The trap piece should be about 3 x 1⅛ inches. Set a half-inch round-head wood screw as shown in the illustration, screwing it part way in, leaving it out just as far as the width of your trap piece. Drill a hole in your trap piece just big enough to fit over the head of the screw. Set the screw so that the trap piece can move freely but with a minimum of play. (An alternative method is to drill through the trap piece and through the wood and place a bolt. Tighten the nut, then loosen it just enough that the trap will drop freely over the entrance.) Place a second wood screw as a stopper for the trap piece when the trap is tripped, as shown in the illustration. The screw should be driven just far enough that the trap piece falls in behind the head. A roofing nail makes a good alternative stopper.

With a piece of coat hanger or other stiff wire, bend your trigger piece as shown, and staple it into place with staples loose enough that the wire can readily turn within them. When a sparrow enters the box, it hops down onto the loop and springs the trap.

This trap can be fastened inside the front of a standard bluebird box with wood screws. It is best adapted to the Huber flip flop box, where the front simply flops down out of the way and the trap replaces it. If you would like to build one of these boxes, see Huber's diagram for construction.

Joe Huber's latest system is to build a trap into each box that he makes. He leaves the trap piece out; the rest of his trap does not interfere with nesting. With a trap piece that will fit over the wood screw head, he can easily put one in when he needs to catch a sparrow. By controlling the house sparrows, he has been able to get bluebirds to nest in the city.

Stutchbury sparrow trap

A Huber trap cannot be used with a slot entrance box. Fortunately, a remarkably simple trap for catching birds in a nesting box has been developed that will work on either type of entrance. Stutchbury and Robertson (1986) invented the trap for capturing tree swallows in their study of this species in Ontario.

Figure 11. Stutchbury sparrow trap

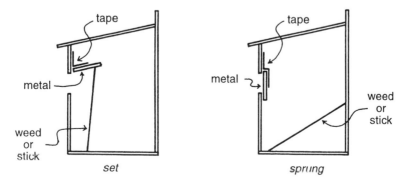

A flat piece of aluminum about 6 x 6 cm is suspended over the entrance hole on the inside of the box, with two pieces of masking tape running from above the entrance down onto the back of the aluminum. The tape makes a hinge when the aluminum is lifted to open the entrance. The trap is help up with a thin stick or a stiff piece of grass. When a bird enters the box, it knocks away the support and the trap falls over the entrance.

House sparrows have a tendency to lift the trap and escape. The trap should work well in the Peterson box because of the forward slant of the front.

We thought the trap would work better if it were larger and heavier, so we made the following modifications. Cut a piece of glass (Plexiglas can be cut on your table saw), sheet metal, or plastic about half an inch less than the width of your slot entrance and about two inches wide. Run a piece of tape (duct, adhesive, or masking) from the underside of the roof onto your trap so that the trap hangs down just inside the entrance, blocking it. Use thumb tacks to fasten the tape firmly to the roof.

To set the trap, prop it against the roof with a piece of straw or weed just strong enough to hold up the trap. The straw will run from the trap piece to the floor of the box. When a sparrow enters the box, it knocks the straw away and the trap drops. You may want to tape a quarter or a large washer to the bottom edge of the trap in such a way that it will be on the inside when the trap is sprung. This adds weight to the trap and makes it less likely that the sparrow can escape. This trap is more likely to be effective if the box can be tilted forward before the trap is set. Of course, a trap set for sparrows should be monitored closely so that if you do catch a bluebird it can be released quickly.

If you wish to build a special box for trapping sparrows, you can exclude bluebirds by making the slot entrance only one inch (25 mm) high. Make the box six inches or more from entrance to floor and six inches from front to back. This will allow you to make your trap about four inches long so that it hangs down well below the entrance making it less likely that the sparrow can escape.

Raccoon guards

If predators, especially raccoons, are a problem at your bluebird boxes, you can try to build out unwanted visitors. A variety of methods and gadgets has been tried to keep a raccoon from reaching into a box and getting to eggs and young. Unfortunately, if such a device will foil a raccoon, it is usually rejected by the bluebirds. Some success has been derived by putting a gadget on after the eggs are laid and the birds have a strong desire to enter.

I do not begrudge the raccoons an occasional meal and thus do not worry about them on my bluebird trails. I sometimes move a box that is too close to the water and raided too often, but otherwise I leave the raccoons alone. I realize, however, that in some areas raccoons are so abundant and persistent that if nothing is done a good trail could scarcely raise any bluebirds. Also I realize that a person who has bluebirds nesting in the yard and enjoys watching them from the house will want to go to some effort to provide permanent protection from raccoons and cats. It can be done.

The simplest method of foiling raccoons is to mount boxes on an iron pipe and give the pipe a generous coating of a mixture of five pounds of chassis grease and a quart of turpentine. Gilbertson mounts boxes on electric conduit smoothed with coarse steel wool and polished with carnauba car wax. Neither method is foolproof; occasionally raccoons will go through the grease and some individuals can climb the smoothest pipe.

Noel raccoon guard. Jim Noel developed a raccoon guard that some people have found useful. With a piece of hardware cloth and some staples, follow the drawing below.

Cut and bend the hardware cloth as illustrated. When the mesh is properly folded, it will form a 3½ x 5½-inch box. Fit the wire structure over the opening of the nest box with the 3½-inch cut at the top above the nest box opening and staple to the door along the 5½-inch sides. Be sure to bend the wires on the raw edge (the edge that points toward you as you approach the box) away from the nest box opening.

This design is meant to fit the Peterson box or any other with a

Figure 12. Noel raccoon guard

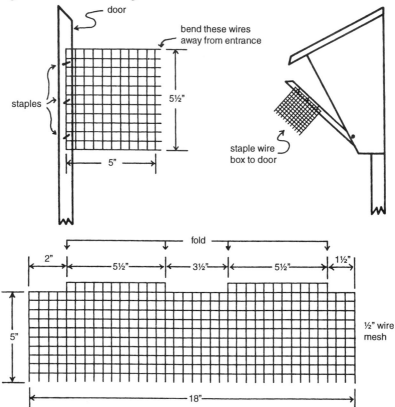

circular entrance and a front 3½ inches wide. A nice modification is to fasten your Noel guards to loose pieces of wood with 1½-inch entrance holes and then fasten these onto the front of your nest boxes as needed. Although some people have been pleased with the Noel guard, several others have reported that raccoons have raided some boxes with guards, especially some of the shallow Peterson boxes.

Conical raccoon guard. Sheet metal wrapped around a post is not effective as a raccoon deterrent; raccoons have no trouble climbing such a post. This conical guard, however, will foil some of your predators. Do not use aluminum sheeting; raccoons and even the wind will

Figure 13. Conical raccoon guard

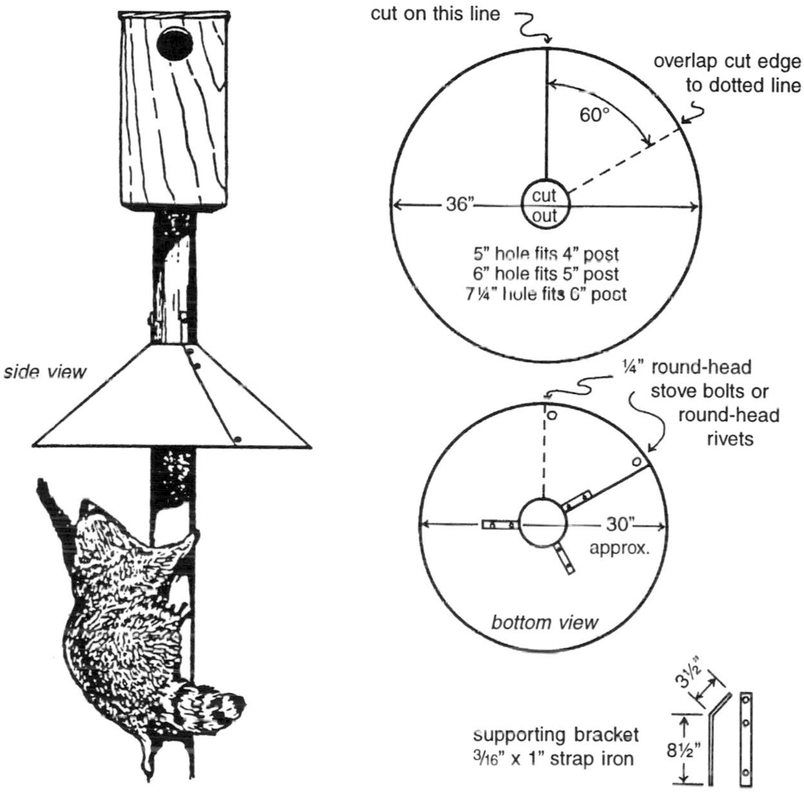

cut on this line

overlap cut edge
to dotted line

60°

36"

cut
out

5" hole fits 4" post
6" hole fits 5" post
7¼" hole fits 6" post

side view

¼" round-head
stove bolts or
round-head
rivets

30"
approx.

bottom view

supporting bracket
³⁄₁₆" x 1" strap iron

3½"

8½"

tear it up. All you need to build this guard is galvanized sheet metal—the kind used for making ducts, available from heating and air conditioning suppliers—and strap iron for supporting brackets (wooden blocks may be used instead).

Cut a piece of galvanized sheet metal thirty-six inches in diameter. Cut a line for making the cone and a hole in the center following the measurements shown on the diagram. Secure the cone with quarter-inch round-head stove bolts or round-head rivets and install the supporting brackets to mount the cone on your pole.

Curtis Dew found a simpler method than attaching a cone to the pole. He places a piece of sheet metal three feet square directly under the box. From the building supply store get a threaded iron pipe three-quarters of an inch in diameter, a floor plate to fit it, and a piece of rebar three feet long to fit inside the pipe. To construct Dew's guard, make a false bottom for your bluebird box using a 1½-inch thick piece of wood. Fasten it in place so that it extends slightly below the bottom of the front door; be sure the door will open. Draw diagonal lines from the corners of your sheet metal to locate the center. Place the floor plate in the center and drill holes through the sheet metal and into the false floor of your box. Screw the floor plate and sheet metal to the bottom of the box.

At the place you want to put your box drive the metal rod (rebar) about halfway into the ground taking care to assure that it is straight; you may want to use a level or a plumb bob. Put the end of your pipe over the rod. With a piece of wood over the top of the pipe to prevent battering of the threads drive the pipe into the ground about a foot until it is solid. Finally screw the floor plate with attached sheet metal and bluebird box onto the pipe. Your box is now about as safe from predators as you can make it. Of course, like all bluebird boxes, it should be out in the open where cats and squirrels cannot leap to it from branches or buildings. One of the advantages of this type of mounting is that the entire system is easily moved to another location.

Snake trap

Harry Krueger designed a very effective snake trap using netting available at garden shops for keeping birds out of your berry patch. You can construct this simple contraption in minutes using the netting, 12 gauge galvanized wire, and 24 gauge galvanized or copper wire. Make a circle sixteen inches in diameter from the 12 gauge wire, overlap the wire two inches, and wrap the splice with 24 gauge wire. Now cut the garden net and wire the long edge onto the wire loop by wrapping with the 24 gauge wire every four inches. Gather the net at the middle and wire it tightly to the pole. The net should stand out from the support pole, making a skirt to trap the snakes.

A simpler plan than that which is illustrated is also effective; you do not need the ring of wire at the bottom. Any arrangement

Figure 14. Snake trap

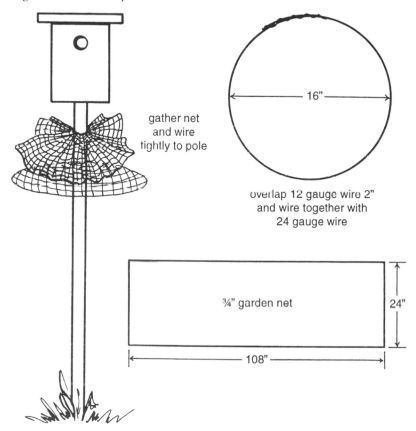

gather net
and wire
tightly to pole

16"

overlap 12 gauge wire 2"
and wire together with
24 gauge wire

¾" garden net

24"

108"

whereby a snake climbs the pole, comes under the netting, and must go through several layers will catch the snake. Wrap your netting at least twice around the pole, very loosely, so that it will billow out at the bottom and the top. Tie it in the middle to the pole. With a snake trap in place, you must check the station every morning. Bluebirds will be frightened by a snake in the trap and probably will not enter the box until the snake is removed.

The advantage of this trap is that, if you do not want to kill snakes, they can be cut loose and freed somewhere away from your trail.

Tuttle cattle guard

Although pasture is excellent bluebird habitat, boxes cannot be placed where they are accessible to cattle, for the animals will rub on them and destroy them. It may be necessary, however, to situate boxes away from a brushy or woodsy fence row to avoid problems with wrens, flying squirrels, and snakes. Richard Tuttle has designed a method for placing boxes in open pasture. A ring of barbed wire deters cattle.

Figure 15. Tuttle's steel livestock guard

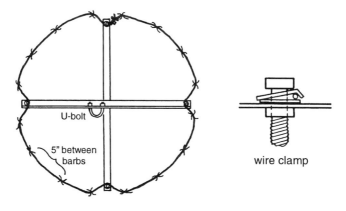

To construct Tuttle's steel livestock guard, prepare two pieces of ⅛ x 1 x 1-inch angle iron twenty-four inches long. Weld or bolt the two pieces together to make a cross. Drill a quarter-inch hole in the end of each cross member to hold a wire clamp. Drill two holes in the cross and install a U-bolt that will serve to attach the guard to a pipe mount. Construct wire clamps from ¼ x 1-inch bolts and ⅜- and ⁵⁄₁₆-inch washers. For three of the clamps, put a lip on the ⅜-inch washers. Assemble the wire clamps as shown in the illustration and fit them into the holes in the ends of the cross members. The fourth wire clamp holds the overlapped barbed wire; put two lips on opposite sides of the ⅜-inch washer and assemble in the remaining hole in the cross member.

Use at least eighty-five inches of 12½ gauge barbed wire with five-inch spacing. Each quarter circle of the guard has twenty inches of wire with four barbs. Clamp the barbed wire in each of the wire clamps so that the barbed wire forms a circle around the cross. Overlap the ends of the barbed wire on the fourth clamp so that one wire rests on either side of the bolt and twist the ends around the wire.

Figure 16. Tuttle's wooden livestock guard

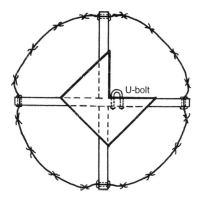

To construct Tuttle's livestock guard out of wood, prepare a piece of outdoor plywood ¾ x 8 x 8 inches with one-quarter of it cut out as shown in the illustration above. Glue and nail one piece of white pine one-by-two twenty-four inches long and two pieces of white pine one-by-two 11⅝ inches long to the center support to make a cross. (Glue the one-inch side to the center support.) Drill a hole in the end of each cross member for attaching the wire. Drill two holes in a cross member and install a U-bolt that will serve to attach the guard to a pipe mount. Use at least eighty-five inches of 12½ gauge barbed wire with five-inch spacing. The ends of the barbed wire will be overlapped and joined to form a circle. Each quarter-circle of the guard has twenty inches of wire with four barbs. Insert a six-inch piece of 12 gauge wire in the hole in the end of each cross member and wrap each end of the wire for two revolutions around the barbed wire to produce a snug fit. Bend the end of each wire to produce additional barbs.

Whether you are building the steel livestock guard or the wooden one, paint the guard with a color that *contrasts* with the foliage in order to deter collisions.

Bell's system for hanging boxes on utility poles

To attach bluebird nest boxes to utility poles, with the permission of the utility companies, Ralph Bell has developed a system. He drills a hole through each side of the box near the back and just beneath the roof. A wire is then strung through the box and around the pole. A single roofing nail is driven into the pole on the side opposite the box. The head of the nail protrudes only about a quarter of an inch. The box hangs against the pole suspended by the wire. If a lineman needs to climb a pole, he simply lifts the wire off the nail and drops the box to the ground.

Building boxes, guards, and feeders for bluebirds is simple, inexpensive, and gives you something to do on a rainy day. With a few materials and tools, you'll be able to build much better structures than are available commercially.

____ 12 ____
Photographing Birds

BLUEBIRDS ARE IDEAL SUBJECTS for bird photography, for beginners as well as experienced photographers. They
are beautiful, and the colorful male assists in feeding the young, so he
will be available to pose for you.

Boxes can be placed with photography in mind. Consider the
position of the sun, the time of day you will be working, and the background you want. If feasible, plan to have several bluebird families
available. Because of individual variation in behavior, some birds are
shy and others are bold. If one pair doesn't cooperate readily, try
another.

Bluebirds are excellent subjects for photography.

A bird can be "posed."

Bluebirds are remarkably tolerant of disturbance. If a box with young birds is not in the best position, move it. Even if there are young in a box, you can move it from one post to the next. The parents will be upset at first but will recognize the new location and usually regain normal behavior within a couple of hours. If you want to photograph a different kind of box than the one the nest is in or one built especially for photography, remove the nest box, put the nest in your new box, and erect it in the position you want for photographing.

If you want pictures of bluebirds without a nest box, such as a perched bird with the sky as a background, place a box in the open where there is no fence or other nearby perch. Set an old fence post or whatever you want your bird to alight on close to the box and wait for the bird to settle there.

To get good photos, you must be patient and observe your birds in the course of their normal activities without causing them stress or fear. This means you must hide the camera and photographer. For this, a good blind is essential.

The Blind

Any of several structures can serve as a blind: a car, a house, a tent, a pickup truck with a camper, a playhouse in the yard, or a structure built especially for photography. For a blind to be satisfactory, it must be comfortable enough for the photographer to spend several hours at a time, allow for several shooting angles, acceptable to the birds, resistant to wind, and either hidden from people or arranged in such a way or place that people will not bother you while you are working.

To make the blind acceptable to birds, it must be lightproof or camouflaged so that the birds do not see the photographer. Plan to take two or three days to get the blind in position and ready for use. Set up about forty-five feet from the box you plan to photograph. Put a bottle into the blind where your camera will be to serve as a dummy

The blind

lens. Leave the blind in place for a couple of days to give the wildlife a chance to become accustomed to it.

Bring the blind to working distance on the third day. You can get pretty close, but respect the tolerance level of the birds. Get in and out of the blind without being seen by the birds so that they do not associate the blind with danger. If the parents stay so close that this is not feasible, have a friend walk up to the blind with you. Enter the blind while the friend walks around a bit, then leaves. Birds apparently cannot count and will accept the blind as empty.

Have a comfortable chair in your blind; you can expect to spend time just waiting. Take in something to drink and a snack. Bring a notebook to record interesting observations. Various other things that you may need to take interesting photos include tape, knife, screwdriver, brush, tissues, safety pins, and flashlight.

Once you are in the blind, do not take pictures for the first ten minutes or so. The parents may feel that something is different, so let them come and feed two or three times to reestablish their normal

Standard equipment

A bird's eye view from inside the nesting box

ritual. Use this time to watch their habits and to calculate what kind
of pictures are likely to become available to you. Make sure that all of
your equipment is set up and ready to work. Then double check. If
the birds don't enter the box within an hour, back off and wait an
extra day.

Equipment

A 35 mm camera is recommended for photographing birds. It is ver-
satile, lightweight, has bright reflex viewing, a range of shutter speeds
up to 1000th of a second, and a lens that can be easily changed. Most
important, what you see is what you record on your film. The lens
you want is a 300, with or without an extension tube; 180 is also good.
The lens you choose depends upon the distance to the bird and how
tight you want the photograph to be. Sometimes you'll want a general photo of the bird and its surroundings, and other times you'll be

Snapping a bird in flight takes patience.

trying for a close-up portrait. To include the habitat in your photo, use a wider angle lens.

A motor is essential when photographing birds. A lot of things can happen quickly and you won't want to take your eye off the viewfinder. A motor will advance the film automatically after you take a photo.

A tripod and a cable release are important for getting good pictures.

You may want to use a remote control for your camera. You can choose an air release, which works effectively over a short range. An electrical release will allow you to work from a greater distance. The ultimate system is a radio release, which is expensive. There are advantages and disadvantages to photographing with a remote release. The major advantage is that it is easier to camouflage a camera and tripod and get the birds accustomed to a fake setup than it is to build a blind. A major disadvantage is that you cannot see what is in your

Pest or guest?

frame; you cannot compose the picture you want. The focus is also a critical problem. With a remote, you will need to use a shorter tele-photo lens, which will give you better coverage and a greater depth of field.

For film, I recommend Fugichrome 100 or Kodachrome 64 for sunny days. On overcast days, use 200 Kodachrome. If you want to take black and white photos, choose T. Max 100 or 400 or Ilford FP4 or HP5.

Setting Up Your Shots

When you are setting up a shot, nothing should be visible very close behind the box. Remember that you can move the box if necessary. It is always better to have a tree in the background than the sky. Think about what is going to be in the background before you set up the photograph.

The sun is very important. On a sunny day it is better to photo-graph early in the morning (before 10:00) and late in the afternoon (after 5:30) than during the middle of the day. You may sometimes need to tilt the box a little to avoid shadows from the roof.

Photographs taken with natural light are best. Plan to take your pictures when the sun is behind you and lighting the box. If the light is constant, meter the grass and keep that rating. Give priority to shut-ter speed over F stop.

Sometimes you may need to fill in with artificial light. With shut-ter speed set at $1/60$ second, set up an automatic flash one F stop less than the F stop on your lens. Avoid using more than one flash; you will put too many highlights in the bird's eyes, giving an artificial flavor to your pictures. The birds quickly become accustomed to the flash.

You will need to build a fake tripod and camera and put them close to the box and allow enough time for the birds to become accus-tomed to them. This arrangement does not need to be elaborate; three sticks tied together with a cardboard box on top will do. You may want to set a post near the box for the birds to land on so that you can get pictures of them perched and carrying food for the young.

Different focuses

When you set up your real tripod and camera, hang a weight from the center column to maximize stability. Put your mirror up and try to cover the viewfinder since your body will not be blocking the light. I use a remote to get a clear angle to the scene. I set up the blind in front of the box, where I can observe the normal behavior of the birds. I set up the camera and tripod off to the side.

Birds in Flight

To photograph your birds in flight, you will need a very fast shutter speed—$1/1000$ or $1/2000$ of a second. Watch the flight pattern as your birds approach the box, and set up the camera to catch them just before they land. Prefocus, and shoot when the bird enters the frame. Put your camera and tripod to the side of the box; side shots are easier and usually preferable to head-on.

_____ 13 _____
Troubleshooting

Q: I have had a box up throughout the spring and nothing is using it. What is wrong?

A: Check the site and habitat. Bluebirds prefer boxes on posts or poles to those on trees. The box must be in the open and not obstructed by vines or leaves. There must be some open habitat where the birds can forage.

Keep checking your box regularly and keep it free of ants and wasps. Some bluebirds are shy and seldom seen; there may be a nest in the box and you didn't realize it. Consider putting up more boxes. If your box has a circular entrance build some slot entrance boxes, which bluebirds prefer. Even in the best of habitat, some boxes may not be used. If you have a dozen boxes scattered over good habitat, you are almost certain to get bluebirds unless a severe winter in the southern states has nearly eliminated the population.

If your box is not used the first year, do not give up. In many cases where we have had unused boxes in good habitat, bluebirds have moved in the second year.

Q: The bluebirds came, explored the box with obvious excitement, then left and didn't return. What caused this?

A: This behavior is not a problem; it is very common, especially in early spring. The birds may not return for a month or more, but they probably will nest in your box. They have staked out their nest site but are waiting for more dependable weather and a better supply of insects before starting a family. If bluebirds start too early, the first brood often starves in the box. If you inspect your box carefully, you are likely to find a trace of nesting material, often a single fine strand of dried grass. This seems to be a claims marker; such a marked box is nearly always used later in the season.

Q: Bluebirds started a nest in my box but didn't finish it. Why?
A: They probably will finish it. It is common for bluebirds to start a nest and then leave it untouched for a month or more before completing it, especially if it was started in early spring. Here again they have claimed their site and are simply waiting for optimum conditions. Bluebirds will occasionally start a nest and actually abandon it, especially if you have other boxes in the vicinity. Sometimes they find another site more to their liking and move after they have started to build a nest.

Q: My bluebirds built a nice neat nest and then never used it. Why not?
A: The situation is probably similar to the one described above. Bluebirds will commonly build a nice nest right away and then wait a month or more before laying eggs. We once had a pair build a nest in April and not lay eggs until July. If the surface of the nest cup is messed up, however, the nest has been abandoned.

Q: What causes these messed up nests, and what should I do about them?
A: A raccoon is nearly always the cause of this fairly common problem. Such nests are never used and should be removed as soon as discovered. The bluebirds will nearly always build again. You should consider trying to make the box safe from raccoons.

Q: I had a nest with five eggs, and the next time I checked it there was only one. A few days later there were five. What was going on?
A: Your nest was raided by a snake, most likely the black rat snake (*Elaphe obsoleta*). The snake removes the eggs without disturbing the nest or leaving any other sign of its visit. The bluebirds simply lay again and often raise a brood without another visit from the snake. Young birds that appear to have fledged earlier than expected have often become the victims of snake activity. Within the geographic range

of the rat snake it is often the most serious predator at bluebird nests and the most difficult one to discourage. Try moving your box at least one hundred yards from any woods, old hollow trees, and buildings. See the section on snakes in chapter 9, Predators.

Q: Each of the bluebird eggs in my nest box had been punctured, as if with a needle. What causes this?
A: A house wren. Clean out your box and move it farther from the woods and brush. Male house sparrows occasionally will enter a box and peck a hole in an egg. There is no way to prevent this.

Q: What causes a box to be filled with sticks?
A: A house wren. Although house wrens are a nuisance on the bluebird trail, they are native songbirds and are protected by state and federal laws. It is unlawful to destroy their nests.

Q: I opened my nest box, and ants came swarming out. What should I do?
A: If there are live young, fashion a crude cup from dry grass and remove the young from the box. Put them in the cup and place it on the ground in the shade. With a large screwdriver, remove the nest from the box. Spray the box lightly with a household bug bomb, preferably one whose active ingredients are pyrethrins and petroleum distillate. (From a pet shop you can obtain a spray made for use on cage birds.) Spray the old nest. As the ants in the box die, scrape them out along with the eggs and pupae. When the box is free of ants, put the young and the new nest you constructed in the box. An alternative is to simply replace the infested box. For more on keeping ants away from your boxes, see the section on ants, chapter 7, Guests and Pests.

Q: When there are eggs in a nest how do I tell if it is active or abandoned?
A: In an active nest the nest cup is neat and smooth and the eggs stand out free on top of the nest material. If the eggs are partially worked down into the nest material or have some dry grass on top of

them, they have been abandoned. If a completed clutch has been in the box for three weeks or more, you should suspect abandonment. Feel the eggs to see if they are warm. Take the eggs out one at a time and examine them. See if they are cracked or show dark through the shell, or if they smell rotten. Do not hesitate to examine eggs. Bluebirds are very tolerant of human disturbance and will not abandon because of it.

Bluebirds will build a new nest over abandoned eggs. If you are sure a clutch is abandoned, however, it is probably best to remove the nest and eggs; the birds are more likely to start a new nest in the box if it is empty.

Q: What should I do when young are abandoned in the nest?
A: First, make sure they are abandoned. Even feathers or a dead parent on the ground may not be proof; a single parent can raise the brood. Watch the box for half an hour or place a piece of grass in the entrance or spider web across the entrance. If a young bird is near death, cup it in your hands to warm it, then feed it. Insects, slugs, or sow bugs (found under rocks), canned dog or cat food, ground beef, or mealworms (available at your pet store) will be eaten. Once In early spring when I couldn't find insects, I revived an orphan with aquatic snails that I mashed and removed shell fragments from.

As soon as your orphan has recovered, foster it into another brood of about the same age. You should not try to raise a young bird yourself. They need to be fed at least once every twenty minutes from dawn to dusk, a most demanding task. To do it legally, you would need to obtain federal and state permits. If you decide to do it anyway, read the chapter on foster-parenting bluebirds in Zeleny (1976).

Q: Everything was going fine, then the babies just disappeared. They surely weren't yet able to fly. What happened?
A: A snake has visited the box. See the section on snakes in chapter 9, Predators.

Q: Something took the young, messed up the nest, and left bluebird feathers on the ground. What was it?

A: There are several possibilities, the most likely of which is a raccoon or a house cat.

Q: Something killed an adult bluebird at the box. Feathers on the top and back of the head were gone and the skull was bloody. What did this?

A: A house sparrow. They may kill either the male or female, often in the box, but sometimes on the ground. They may throw small young birds out or kill larger ones in the nest.

Solve the problem by putting up a slot entrance box with a floor only about three to four inches below the entrance. The surviving adult bluebird is likely to get a new mate and move into this one. Leave the raided box in place, but clean it out. If house sparrows build in it, trap them with a Huber trap and destroy them, or remove their nest and place blocks of wood in the box to make it more shallow (no less than three inches).

Another way to deal with house sparrows is to remove the nest, put a sticky mouse trap in the box, then watch until the sparrow enters. Kill it by squeezing the breast with a finger beneath each wing. If you catch the male (the one with the black throat), you have solved the problem.

An alternative is to allow sparrows to build their nest, then remove their eggs when the normal clutch of five is complete; the sparrows will usually abandon. Never allow house sparrows to raise young in a bluebird house. Successful nesting will lead to the evolution of a population of house sparrows adapted to breeding in bluebird boxes, making our problems worse in future years.

Q: The young were over half grown and then they all died. What caused this?

A: This is common with the first broods when we have a cool rainy spring. Zeleny (1993) has shown that the usual cause of this mortality is chilling at night. Parents may have trouble foraging in the rain and finding enough food. The larger the young the more food they require and the more susceptible they are to this death pattern. Broods nearly ready to fledge are often found dead in the box. If a small young bird dies it is removed by the parents. With larger young, however, when one dies they usually all do. Remove the dead young and the nest. Your bluebirds will almost certainly nest again.

Occasionally nestlings will die of heat during extremely hot weather. If the temperature goes above 95 degrees Fahrenheit, check on your young birds. You may want to leave the door partially open to improve ventilation. If your box is not adequately ventilated, you can take it down and transfer nest and young to one that is. Richard Tuttle has designed a well ventilated box by making the back a quarter of an inch shorter than the sides leaving a quarter-inch slot at the back beneath the roof. This with a slot entrance box gives excellent cross circulation. You can drill two holes through the back or through the sides and wire the box to a fence.

Q: A mockingbird took over my yard and drove the bluebirds away. How can I prevent that?
A: There is no legal way that we know. Mockingbirds are protected by law. There are numerous reports of mockingbirds being aggressive toward bluebirds (Blackburn 1990), in some cases even to the point of not allowing the bluebirds to feed their young in the box (Berner et al. 1992). Fortunately, this is not a very common occurrence. Mockingbirds are common along all our bluebird trails in Kentucky, and we have never seen any problems with them.

Q: Should I remove old nests from the box?
A: If you are talking about between broods in one season, it doesn't make much difference; the bluebirds will return for a second brood whether the box is cleaned or not. An old nest may encourage ants. If there are mouse nests in the boxes, these should definitely be cleaned out by early spring. Although all writers on monitoring bluebird trails recommend removing used bluebird nests, there is serious question as to whether this should be done. Though an old nest may encourage ants, Mason (1944) reported on the minute wasps that parasitize and kill the pupae of the blowflies, which feed on the blood of nestlings; they overwinter as larvae in the old nest and emerge as adults in late spring and early summer. Mason believed that the enormous

populations of blowfly larvae in his boxes were the result of years of trail management and his habit of removing old nests. Our research has shown that, given a choice, bluebirds have a strong preference for building onto an old nest rather than in a clean box. Thus, unless the old nests are taking up too much space it is probably best not to remove them.

Q: What should I do about wasps?
A: Wasps aren't really the problem that they seem to be. They don't seem to bother the bluebirds; they appear later in the season and build nests usually beneath the roof, but sometimes on the sides, of unused boxes. The wasp nest is easily dislodged with a screwdriver, and the wasps are not aggressive. If you are afraid of the wasps, come back at night to dislodge them.

Appendix

Organizations and Suppliers

Ahlgren Construction
14017 Whiterock Road
Burnsville, Minnesota 55337
Provides a Jim Noel type raccoon guard; designed for the Peterson box, it could be modified for use on a slot entrance box. Builds and sells Peterson nest boxes.

Bat Conservation International
P.O. Box 162603
Austin, Texas 78716

Bluebirds Across Vermont
Steven G. Parren
Vermont Fish and Wildlife
324 North Main Street
Barre, Vermont 05641
A statewide bluebird network established by the Vermont Audubon Council.

Bluebird Association of Maine
Esther Leck
Wiscasset, Maine

Bluebirds Over Georgia
Box 53344
Atlanta, Georgia 30355

Bluebird Recovery Program
Audubon Chapter of Minneapolis
Box 3801
Minneapolis, Minnesota 55403
Provides many materials and services. Publishes quarterly Bluebird News. *Yearly subscription, $5.00.*

Bluebird Restoration Association of Wisconsin
Delores Wendt, Treasurer
1751 28th Avenue
Rice Lake, Wisconsin 54868
Annual meeting. Sales of various items. Publishes quarterly Wisconsin Bluebird. *Yearly subscription, $5.00.*

Cedar Valley Live Traps
7441 100th Street Circle
Bloomington, Minnesota 55438
Sells a good multiple-catch sparrow trap.

Dahlem Enviromental Education Center
7117 S. Jackson Road
Jackson, Michigan 49201
Sponsors an annual bluebird festival.

Dakota Wildlife Trust Bluebird Recovery Team
Box 572
Valley City, North Dakota 58072

Georgia Mealies
Rt. 7, Box 508
Tifton, Georgia 32794
Mealworm supplier.

Steve Gilbertson
3521 135th Lane NW
Andover, Minnesota 55304
For $5.00 he will send you his trap for catching sparrows in a bluebird box. He will also provide his PVC sparrow resistant box.

Grubco, Inc.
Box 15001
Hamilton, Ohio 45015
Quantity supplies of mealworms.

Herd-A-Bird
Mark Wallace
10537 Martellini Drive
Laurel, Maryland 20723
Sells a large multicapture trap for control of house sparrows, $85.

Homes for Bluebirds, Inc.
Jack R. Finch
Rt. 1 Box 341
Bailey, North Carolina 27807
Provider of nest boxes and feeder boxes. Has a dogwood orchard from which he gathers dogwood berries for feeding bluebirds in winter. Will sell feeders and provide a pamphlet on feeding bluebirds.

Joe Huber
1720 Evergreen Court
Heath, Ohio 43056
He will provide a Huber sparrow trap in a box, $18.00.

Illinois Department of Conservation
Natural Heritage Division
524 South Second Street
Springfield, Illinois 62706
Holds annual bluebird workshops throughout the state and coordinates volunteer efforts to reestablish bluebirds in Illinois.

Iowa Bluebird Recovery Program
c/o Sac County Conservation Foundation
Rt. 3, Box 96A
Sac City, Iowa 51433
Annual meeting.

Jackson Audubon Society Bluebird Project
Reber Layton
Box 12157
Jackson, Mississippi 39211
Their remarkable activity has resulted in over 36,000 bluebird boxes being distributed throughout the state. Their boxes have been available at various retail outlets in villages throughout Mississippi.

The Nature Society
Purple Martin Junction
Griggsville, Illinois 62340
Publishes the monthly Nature Society News. *Mostly about purple martins (formerly* Purple Martin News) *but always has something about bluebirds. Yearly subscription, $12.00.*

North American Bluebird Society
Box 6295
Silver Spring, Maryland 20906-0295
For anyone with an interest in bluebirds. Dues, $15.00 a year for a regular membership, $10.00 for students under twenty-one and seniors over sixty. Includes a subscription to the quarterly journal Sialia, *which provides informative articles and news about the world of bluebirds. Each issue includes an order blank for purchasing dozens of items concerning bluebirds.*

North Carolina Bluebird Society
Box 4191
Greensboro, North Carolina 27404
Publishes Bluebird Notes.

Ohio Bluebird Society
11669 State Park Road
Athens, Ohio 45701
Holds annual meetings. Publishes the Bluebird Monitor *quarterly. Annual membership, $10.00.*

Ontario Bluebird Society
William F. Reed
165 Green Valley Drive #2
Kitchener, Ontario, Canada N2D 1K3

The Tanglefoot Company
314 Straight Avenue SW
Grand Rapids, Michigan 49504
Suppliers of Tangle Trap, useful for keeping ants from invading your bluebird boxes. Your farm or garden supply store can also order it for you.

Andrew Troyer
Rt. 3, Box 72
Conneautville, Pennsylvania 16406
He provides a plan for his large walk-in trap for house sparrows and starlings, $6.00.

Upstate New York Bluebird Society
Ray Briggs, President
Rt 1
Cobbleskill, New York 12043

Wild Birds Unlimited
A chain of retail stores providing materials for people interested in birds, they carry an excellent assortment of materials concerning bluebirds. If an outlet is near you, you may want to shop there instead of ordering by mail. Wild Birds Unlimited is growing as rapidly as the interest in bluebirds and now has outlets in Alabama, Colorado, Connecticut, Florida, Illinois, Indiana, Kentucky, Maryland, Massachusetts, Michigan, Missouri, New York, North Carolina, Ohio, Oklahoma, Pennsylvania, Tennessee, and Wisconsin.

Literature Cited

Abbey, B. 1993. Bluebird news from around the state. *Bluebird Notes* 8 (1): 2.

Barber, T.A. 1990. Seven eastern bluebird nestlings in one box. *Sialia* 12:110-11.

Bart, J. 1977. Impact of human visitation on avian nesting success. *Living Bird* 16:187-92.

Bart, J., and D.S. Robson. 1982. Estimating survivorship where subjects are visited periodically. *Ecology* 63:1078-90.

Baxter, J.R. 1982. House sparrows shun this nesting box. *Sialia* 4:137-38.

Berner, K.L. 1990. Field test of predator-deterrent nest box devices for acceptance by cavity-nesting birds. *Sialia* 12:123-28.

Berner, K.L. 1991. Field tests of the "Bird Guardian." *Sialia* 13:14-19.

Berner, K.L., and A.S. Mallette. 1993. 1992 nesting box report. *Sialia* 15:45-48.

Berner, K.L., and V.A. Pleines. 1993. Field tests of several styles of bluebird boxes. *Sialia* 15:3-11.

Berner, K.L., D. McGettigan, and S. Krieger. 1990. Testing a raccoon's ability to raid a nest box. *Sialia* 12:83-87.

Berner, K.L., D.J. Clark, F.J. MacDougall, and J. Ambert. 1992. 1991 nesting box report. *Sialia* 14:59-54.

Blackburn, K. 1990. A bird in the bush. *Sialia* 12:63-66.

Bruss, H. 1990. Sparrows and raccoons. *Sialia* 12:103-4.

Caldwell, F.R. 1991. An unlikely suspect. *Bluebird Monitor* 4 (1): 1.

Casses, K. 1992. Too many bluebirds? *Bluebird News* 5 (6): 2.

Cromack, A.S. 1987. Training bluebirds to use a feeder. *Sialia* 9:145.

Curtis, K.E. 1991. My tests of raccoon guards. *Sialia* 13:98, 103.

Darling, D., and J. Thomson-Delaney. 1993. Bluebirds, blowflies, and parasitic wasps. *Sialia* 15:13-16.

Daughrity, C. 1991. Letter. *Sialia* 13:116-17.

Davis, W.H. 1989a. Bluebirds in the Bluegrass prefer wooden boxes. *Sialia* 11:7.

Davis, W.H. 1989b. House sparrows prefer a circular entrance. *Sialia* 11: 8-10.

Davis, W.H. 1989c. Letter to the editor. *Sialia* 11:73.

Davis, W.H. 1991. Foiling house sparrows. *Sialia* 13:51-53.

Davis, W.H., and D. Dourson. 1991. Little brown bat, *Myotis lucifugus*, living in a bluebird box. *Bat Research News* 32:41.

Davis, W.H., and P.J. Kalisz. 1995. Tests of the Peterson box and Zuern's raccoon-inhibiting box. *Sialia* (in press).

Davis, W.H., and K. Mack. 1994. Tests of sparrow-inhibiting boxes. *Sialia* 16:98-99.

Davis, W.H., and W.C. McComb. 1988. Use of Tangle Trap to measure snake predation at bluebird boxes. *Sialia* 10:87-88.

Davis, W.H., and W.C. McComb. 1989. Bluebirds and starlings: competition for nest sites. *Sialia* 11:123-25.

Davis, W.H., W.C. McComb, and P.N. Allaire. 1986. Nest box use by starlings: does it inhibit bluebird production? *Transactions of the Kentucky Academy of Science* 47:133-36.

Davis, W.H., P.J. Kalisz, and R.J. Wells. 1994. Eastern bluebirds prefer boxes containing old nests. *Journal of Field Ornithology* 65:250-53.

Dew, T., C. Dew, and R.B. Layton. 1986. *Bluebirds.* Jackson, Miss.: Nature Books.

Dorber, S. 1988. Presidential points. *Sialia* 10:42.

Dunn, E. 1977. Predation by weasels *(Mustela nivalis)* on breeding tits *(Parus* spp.) in relation to density of tits and rodents. *Journal of Animal Ecology* 46:633-52.

Dupree, D.C. 1988. Raising Mealworms. *Sialia* 10:11-12.

Dupree, D.C., and M. Wright. 1990. 1989 Nesting box report. *Sialia* 12:47-55.

Gilbertson, S.L. 1991. New PVC house attracts bluebirds, not sparrows. *Sialia* 13:93-97.

Gilbertson, S.L. 1993. PVC nest box update. *Sialia* 15:131-35.

Gillis, E. 1989. Western bluebirds, tree swallows and violet-green swallows west of the Cascade Mountains in Oregon, Washington, and Vancouver Island, British Columbia. *Sialia* 11:127-30.

Gowaty, P.A. 1981. Aggression of breeding Eastern Bluebirds *(Sialia sialis)* toward their mates and models of intra-and interspecific intruders. *Animal Behavior* 19:1013-27.

Gowaty, P.A. 1984. House sparrows kill Eastern Bluebirds. *Journal of Field Ornithology* 55: 378-80.

Green, M.M., Jr. 1986. A progress report on a starling-proof winter feeding station for bluebirds. *Sialia* 8:56-59.

Hagerman, D. 1988. Nest box entrance hole preferred by mountain bluebirds. *Sialia* 10:83-86.

Hamilton, W.J. 1943. Nesting of the Eastern Bluebird. *Auk* 60:91-94.

Hanert, K.G. 1991. Question corner. *Sialia* 13: 22.

Hartley, G.L. 1989. Brown-headed nuthatch evicts eastern bluebirds. *Sialia* 11:135.

Havera, S., and N. Havera. 1983. Kestrels prey on nestling bluebirds. *Sialia* 5:93.

Huber, J. 1982. The Joe Huber sparrow trap. *Sialia* 4:20-21.

Huber, J. 1992. Disappearing bluebird eggs? A possible culprit. *Sialia* 14:54-66.

Hurst, G.A. 1991. Feeding station for nestling bluebirds. *Sialia* 13:27.

Hutchings, D. 1991. Guard foils predators. *Sialia* 13:68-69.

Keegan, J. 1988. Letter to the editor. *Sialia* 10:115.

Kennedy, M.L., J.P. Nelson Jr., F.W. Weckerly, D.W. Sugg, and J.C. Stroh. 1991. An assessment of selected forest factors and lake level in raccoon management. *Wildlife Society Bulletin* 19:151-54.

Kingston, R. 1991. Snake/predator guard. *Sialia* 13:56-57.

Kridler, K. 1988. Are PVC nest boxes sparrow resistant? *Sialia* 10:3-6.

Kridler, K. 1991. What to do with house sparrows. *Bluebird News* 4 (5): 2.

Krueger, H. 1989. Fire ant solution. *Sialia* 11:27.

Krueger, H. 1991a. Snake trap. *Sialia* 13:63-67.

Krueger, H. 1991b. Verified fourth nesting by a pair of eastern bluebirds. *Sialia* 13:91-92.

Krueger, H. 1992. Fire ants require special precautions for the bluebirder. *Nature Society News* (April): 12-13.

Laskey, A.R. 1946. Snake predation at bird nests. *Wilson Bulletin* 58:217-18.

Layton, R. 1989. Where are the bluebirds at Christmas time? *Sialia* 11:130-32.

Lippy, K. 1993. Untitled. *Sialia* 15:53.

Lumsden, H.G. 1976. Choice of nest boxes by starlings. *Wilson Bulletin* 88:665-66.

Lumsden, H.G. 1986. Choice of nest boxes by tree swallows, *Tachycineta bicolor*, house wrens, *Troglodytes aedon*, eastern bluebirds, *Sialia sialis*, and European starlings, *Sturnus vulgaris*. *Canadian Field-Naturalist* 100: 343-49.

Lumsden, H.G. 1989. Test of nest box preference of Eastern Bluebirds, *Sialia sialis*, and Tree Swallows, *Tachycineta bicolor*. *Canadian Field-Naturalist* 103:595-97.

Major, R.E. 1990. The effect of human observers on the intensity of nest predation. *Ibis* 132:608-12.

Martin, T.E., and J.J. Roper. 1988. Nest predation and nest site selection in a western population of the Hermit Thrush. *Condor* 90:51-57.

Mason, E.A. 1944. Parasitism by *Protocalliphora* and management of cavity-nesting birds. *Journal of Wildlife Management* 8:232-47.

McComb, W.C., W.H. Davis, and P.N. Allaire. 1987. Excluding starlings from a slot entrance bluebird nest box. *Wildlife Society Bulletin* 15:204-7.

McKinney, R. 1992. What is the talc-like powder left in the nest? *Bluebird News* 5 (4):4.

Meek, S.B., and R.J. Robertson. 1992. How do floater male eastern bluebirds

benefit by filling vacancies on territories where females already have
young? *Behavioral Ecology* 3:95-101.

Moriarty, J.J., and W.H. Davis. 1984. Use of nest boxes on revegetated surface
mines by bat, *Myotis keenii*. *Bat Research News* 25:17-18.

Munro, H.L., and R.C. Rounds. 1985. Selection of artificial nest sites by five
sympatric Passerines. *Journal of Wildlife Management* 49:264-76.

Nichols, J.D., H.F. Percival, R.A. Coon, M.J. Convoy, G.L. Hensler, and J.E.
Hines. 1984. Observer visitation frequency and success of mourning
dove nests: a field experiment. *Auk* 101:398-92.

Noel, J. 1991. Cat and coon guard. *Sialia* 13:58-59.

Olson, C. 1991. Fox predation. *Wisconsin Bluebird* 6 (3): 1-3.

Parren, S.G. 1991. Evaluation of nest-box sites selected by eastern bluebirds,
tree swallows, and house wrens. *Wildlife Society Bulletin* 19:270-77.

Patterson, R.M. 1988. Protecting nesting boxes from climbing predators. *Sialia*
10:15-16, 27.

Peakall, D.B. 1970. The eastern bluebird: its breeding season, clutch size, and
nesting success. *Living Bird* 9:239-55.

Pearman, M. 1991. Avian predation of bluebird nestlings. *Sialia* 13:89-90.

Pinkowski, B.C. 1974. A note on familial longevity in Eastern Bluebirds. *Bird
Banding* 45:363-64.

Pinkowski, B.C. 1975. Yearling male Eastern Bluebird assists parents in feeding young. *Auk* 92:801-2.

Pinkowski, B.C. 1977a. Breeding adaptations in the Eastern Bluebird. *Condor*
79:289-82.

Pinkowski, B.C. 1977b. Blowfly parasitism of Eastern Bluebirds in natural
and artificial nest sites. *Journal of Wildlife Management* 41:272-76.

Pinkowski, B.C. 1978a. Feeding of nestling and fledgling Eastern Bluebirds.
Wilson Bulletin 90:84-98.

Pinkowski, B.C. 1978b. Two successive male Eastern Bluebirds tending to
the same nest. *Auk* 95:606-8.

Pitts, T.D. 1978a. Eastern bluebird mortality at winter roosts in Tennessee.
Bird Banding 49:77-78.

Pitts, T.D. 1978b. Effects of the winter of 1976-1977 on the population size
and reproduction activities of eastern bluebirds in northwest Tennessee during 1977. *Journal of the Tennessee Academy of Science* 53:72.

Pitts, T.D. 1988. Effects of nest box size on Eastern Bluebirds. *Journal of Field
Ornithology* 59:309-13.

Prescott, H.W., and E. Gillis. 1985. An analysis of Western bluebird double
and triple nest box research on Chehalem and Parrett Mountains in
1982. *Sialia* 7:123-30, 146.

Read, W.F. 1989. Nest lowering to prevent raccoon predation. *Sialia* 11:134.

Reed, M.F. 1989. Experiences along a Texas bluebird trail. *Sialia* 11:17-18.

Rendell, W.B., and R.J. Robertson. 1990. Influence of forest edge on nest site selection by Tree Swallows. *Wilson Bulletin* 102:634-44.

Roberts, T.H. 1988. Parasites of the eastern bluebird. *Sialia* 10:28-30.

Roby, D.D., K.L. Brink, and K. Wittmann. 1992. Effects of bird blowfly parasitism on eastern bluebird and tree swallow. *Wilson Bulletin* 104:630-43.

Rounds, R.C., and H.L. Munro. 1983. Broad size of eastern and mountain bluebirds in Manitoba. *Journal of Field Ornithology* 54:304-11.

Sauer, J.R., and S. Droege. 1990. Recent population trends of the Eastern Bluebird. *Wilson Bulletin* 102:239-52.

Schweikert, F. 1988. Letter. *Sialia* 10:72.

Scriven, D.H. 1989. *Bluebirds in the Upper Midwest.* Minneapolis: Bluebird Recovery Committee of the Audubon Chapter of Minneapolis.

Scriven, D.H. 1993. *Bluebird Trails: A Guide to Success.* Minneapolis: Bluebird Recovery Committee of the Audubon Chapter of Minneapolis.

Sedlacek, J.R. 1987. Experimenting with raccoon guards. *Sialia* 9:83-85.

Stroud, P. 1990. Brown-headed nuthatch helps feed bluebird nestlings. *Sialia* 12:136.

Stutchbury, B.J., and R.J. Robertson. 1986. A simple trap for catching birds in nest boxes. *Journal of Field Ornithology* 57:64-65.

Tucker, J.W., Jr. 1990. Male Eastern Bluebird rears four broods during one nesting season. *Wilson Bulletin* 102:726-728.

Tuttle, R.M. 1982. Livestock guards make Bossie, Black Beauty and bluebirds compatible. *Sialia* 4:65-69.

Tuttle, R.M. 1987a. A six year study of nesting tree swallows in Delaware State Park, Delaware, Ohio, 1979-1984. *Sialia* 9:3-7.

Tuttle, R.M. 1987b. A study of winter roost site management and the use of sites by eastern bluebirds in Delaware State Park, Ohio. *Sialia* 9:43-49.

Tuttle, R.M. 1990. Details for a front opening bluebird nest box with a slot entrance. *Sialia* 12:13-15.

Tuttle, R.M. 1991. An analysis of the interspecific competition of Eastern Bluebirds, Tree Swallows, and House Wrens in Delaware State Park, Delaware, Ohio, 1979-1986. *Sialia* 13:3-13.

Wilkins, D. 1992. A potpourri of bluebird theories, observations and comments. *Nature Society News* 27 (7): 12.

Wittmann, K., and R.C. Beason. 1992. The effects of blowfly parasitism on nestling eastern bluebird development. *Journal of Field Ornithology* 63:286-93.

Zeleny, L. 1976. The Bluebird-how you can help its fight for survival. Bloomington: Indiana Univ. Press.

Zeleny, L. 1993. Cold weather may kill bluebird nestlings. *Bluebird Notes* 8 (1): 3.

Zuern, F.A. 1994. Tree branch bluebird box. *Sialia* 16:13-19.

Index

Note: page numbers in bold indicate main headings in text; those in italic indicate photograph or figure accompanying text.